VALUING RELATIONSHIPS

by Tammara Usry

Valuing Relationships
Copyright © 2014
Author: Tammara Usry
Email: monikausry@gmail.com

All scriptures noted in this book were taken from the King James bible unless otherwise noted.

ALL RIGHTS RESERVED. This book contains material protected under International and Federal Copyright Laws and Treaties. Any unauthorized reprint or use of this material is prohibited. No part of this book may be reproduced or transmitted in any form or by any means, electronic or mechanical, including photocopying, recording, or by any information storage and retrieval system without express written permission from the author / publisher.

ISBN-13: 978-0692356371
ISBN-10: 0692356371

Disclaimer: This book is designed to provide information and motivation to our readers. It is sold with the understanding that the publisher is not engaged to render any type of psychological, legal, or any other kind of professional advice. No warranties or guarantees are expressed or implied by the author, since every man has his own measure of faith. The individual author(s) shall not be liable for any physical, psychological, emotional, financial, or commercial damages, including; but not limited to, special, incidental, consequential or other damages. Our views and rights are the same: You are responsible for your own choices, actions, and results.

Dedication

I dedicate this book to my Lord and Savior, Jesus Christ for teaching me what relationship is. Truly, He has shown me what valuing a relationship is through His love and dedication. God, I love you sooo much for sending your only Son, the Great High Priest, Jesus the Christ, to teach me what valuing relationship is and to have a deeper relationship with you through drawing closer to Him. I vow to serve you all of my days and forevermore.

Acknowledgments

I would like to acknowledge many that have contributed to my life, whether small or great. They have given me a clearer understanding of what it means to value a relationship. Everyone mentioned has shown various expressions of love and contributed to my learning to value and cultivate a relationship God's way.

To my husband, Apostle Kerenski Usry: Truly, you have been an amazing and adventurous journey, and I'm so glad that I decided to accept this journey, because it has perfected my perception of the meaning of value. Thank you for your unconditional love, honey. I love you so much my lovey; my booka.

To my Mommy, Lou Anne Simpkins: Thank you for your love and support. Your love is truly incomprehensible at times. I love you.

To my Dad, Thomas Simpkins, Sr: Thank you so much for your love and effort to repair our relationship. Truly, re-exploring this new journey with you has been a delight. I love you and I am looking forward to the latter days being greater than the former.

To my siblings:
My sister, Pamela Taylor
My brothers, Thomas Simpkins Jr, Laranzala Stone, and Jamal Simpkins
I thank you guys for the expressions of your love.
To Apostle Ivory and Evelyn Hopkins: Thank you all for your love, support and willingness to take a chance on us. The sensitivity of the Spirit of the Lord and the impartation that was imparted has forever changed my life for the greater good. The genuineness of your ministry is beyond expressive words. I pray that multiplied grace be given, and that the favor of the Lord will forever be upon your lives...

To Pastor Betty Perez: Thank you for all your love, support, and encouraging words. For there are rare people like yourself. Truly, you are a kind and loving soul. Your ministry has truly demonstrated the love and reconciliation of Christ Jesus. I love you and you're never forgotten. I can testify for many people in your region when I say "*You've been a mom to us all.*" God gave you the right last name: *"Perez"* because your life, presence, love and encouragement has brought breakthrough to many of us. We love you, woman of God.

To Minister Brenda Green: Thank you for all of your love and support. Your radical faith, evangelical thrust, gentleness and kindness is beyond words. Thanks for all your words of encouragement in my desert place. I am truly grateful to you for being there for me, for truly, your words were strength and life to these once broken bones.

To Apostle Linda Thomas Wright: Thank you for all of your support, words of encouragement, words of wisdom and words of correction. For God sent you in a season of me discovering the seer prophetess that I am, and I was truly blessed. The time I spent in your care as a budding prophetess was truly a blessing and it was life changing. At that time, you also strengthened my womanhood and the lifestyle that followed was beyond words. For you understood me and my transitions through the eyes of Christ when no one else did, and made the time to help cultivate me. I send my sincerest gratitude to you for taking me under your wings in the season and years that God sent you into my life. I love you and I valued every moment with you, woman of God.

To Prophetess Michelle Mcclain-Walters: Thank you for all of your words of wisdom, words of correction, and words of encouragement. The time spent in your care, your presence and listening to your advice has forever changed my life for the greater good. I want you to know that your life-giving words are written on my heart like a blueprint that has thrust me into destiny. Your love took a chance on me to teach me a more excellent way, and I'm so grateful for that. Thank you, woman of God.

To Apostles Paul and Doreen Thornton: Thank you for the life-changing impartations and teachings of knowing how to better cultivate a relationship apostolically.

To Apostle Kluane Spake: I thank you so much for coming into my life the time you did, for you have truly impacted my life. Sitting in your presence the first time, let alone the whole weekend, in a one-on-one counseling session, hearing your words of wisdom, words of correction and words of encouragement truly enlightened me of my worth. For truly, that day after leaving your side, my eyes were opened and I gained a new perspective of my own worth. Thank you, woman of God. Those Holy

Spirit inspired words have changed my life and followed me everywhere, even inspiring me to name this book *Valuing Relationships*. Thank you so much for a "due word" in "due season".

To Apostle Jonas Clark: Thank you so much for your guidance, words of wisdom and words of encouragement. You words brought deliverance and an instantaneous change in my life. Truly, meeting you, receiving the impartation and hearing your instructions were needed in the season God sent you.

To Apostle Robert Summers: Thank you for your words of wisdom, guidance, words of encouragement and words of correction, for they broke me free from unhealthy relationships. God knew the right person to send with the deliverance assignment and anointing to break me free from those strongholds that lingered on in my life.

To Prophet Victor Boateng: Thank you for the life-giving words that were spoken that broke things off my life. I thank God for sending you in our region during the season He did, when others who brought you down tried to devalue, discredit and displace me without you knowing it. In that same time, God used you to bring double-honor to me in the presence of my enemies. Thank you for being sensitive to the leading of the Holy Spirit.

To Apostle Marlon Hester: Thank you for your words of wisdom, instructions and words of encouragement. They have given me a greater vision, and I truly appreciate your kindness, man of God.

To Apostle Ronald Phillips: Thank you for your support, words of wisdom and words of encouragement. As I've stated before, your wisdom is underrated, and I pray that this will be the year of acceleration and promotion for you. God bless you, man of God.

To Valerie Walker: Thank you for all your love, hospitality and support. Truly, there was plenty of food at your house. Love you, girly! Your generosity is forever written on my heart, sis.

To Minister Bessie and Papa Willie Danford: Thank you guys for all your love, words of wisdom, discipline and your mentorship. As a budding prophetess, your words helped mold me into who I am today. I love you guys.

To my sister in the Lord, Veronica Seafus: Words can't express the love you've shown me. Your support, words of wisdom, words of encouragement, and words of correction were a delight. It was a privilege to start my journey in the Lord with you. We've had some memorable and exciting times, having each other's backs as mentorees and growing up in the Lord together. I love you, lady. No matter how far we are in distance from each other, we are still unified in Spirit, and when we get together, it's like we were never apart. You are my sister from another mother, but we share the same Heavenly Father, for you are one of a kind, and I'll always love you, sis.

To Jamie Lynn Young (my favorite cousin): I thank you so much for always being there for me, girly. I love you so much for your love, support and honesty. Many will never know the intensity of what we had to experience and endure together, and how much we had (and still have) each other's backs, but girly, I can say we made it. I'm excited about how God will transform your life and bring complete healing to you, but remember, God's grace is sufficient for you. I love you so much, lady. For there's so much more than meets the eye concerning your life, and I'm so excited about the great testimonies ahead regarding your transformation.

To Apostle Yelanda Dyson: I thank you for all of your love, advice, words of encouragement, words of wisdom and support. Truly, your ministry is a ministry of reconciliation. I pray that God will exalt you and the Restorer of Life will bless you beyond measure.

To Prophetess Wanda Best: I want you to know that I thank you for your words of encouragement, words of correction, and words of wisdom. You have shaped me as a woman for the better through the impartation that you gave me and the example that you set for me. Your modesty, conduct and excellence as a woman and wife is beyond words. The times we had together, the laughter, and the good talks were very much cherished. All your love and support as a woman of God and a true example of a virtuous wife to us wives instilled much within me, I thank you for that. Know that much was imprinted on my heart, and remember to never cast away your confidence. I pray that your voice will be heard across the nations and the world will get a chance to hear and see the woman of

God I saw and heard sitting at your table. I love you, woman of God.

To my brother in Christ, Prophet Ricky Watson: Thank you for all of your encouragement, words of wisdom and exhortations. For you are another prophet who is underrated. I pray that this will be a season that God will make your name known all through the world. I love you lil bro, and there's so much more to you than meets the eye.

Prophetess Tiffany Kameni: Thank you so much for your words of encouragement, time, patience and hard work in making this project come alive. I truly appreciate it.

Last, but not least: These ladies have been supportive of me since elementary school, all the way up until unto now: Felicia Oliver, Priscilla Allen, Lashunda Alexander, Martina Lewis, Victoria Prince, Shaquanda Worthen, Erica Braswell, and Chantel Thompson. We are far away from one another and we don't talk on a daily basis, but when we do talk or gather, it's like we were never apart. I love you ladies.

And to anyone who wasn't mentioned, know that you were not forgotten, and there are many more books to come for me to mention you in. I love you.

Table of Contents

Dedication...V
Acknowledgments..VII
Introduction..XIX
Chapter 1..
Introducing "Real Love"...1
Chapter 2..
Rejected Love...7
Chapter 3..
Exploring New Heights of God's Love...................27
Chapter 4..
The Second Love Commandment: "Love your
Neighbor As Yourself"...51
Chapter 5..
Covenant People Versus Divine Connections......59
Chapter 6..
Prophetic Relationships Versus Political
Relationships...81
Chapter 7..
Cultivating Relationships Apostolically.................95
Chapter 8..
Sonship..115
Chapter 9..
Testings of the Relationships..............................129
Chapter 10..
Strengths and Weaknesses.................................135
Chapter 11..
Humility Exposes Pride..139
Chapter 12..
Self-Worth..143

Chapter 13	
Choosing Among Commitments	149
Chapter 14	
False Brethren	159
Chapter 15	
Co-Dependency	163
Chapter 16	
Growing in Wisdom	171
Chapter 17	
Though You May Not Want Me, You Need Me	235
Chapter 18	
Respect & Honor	247
Chapter 19	
Wisdom in Transparency	257
Chapter 20	
Timing	263
Chapter 21	
Corrective Criticism	277
Chapter 22	
Pitfalls in Relationships	281
Chapter 23	
Abuse	297
Chapter 24	
Characteristics of Love	305
Chapter 25	
Quotes	323

Introduction

In this book, I've come to expound on the practical percepts of relationships. There must be a reform to what we call and how we view the vastly different relationships in our lives. My heart longs to see others benefit from the fruitfulness of healthy relationships. Hear my heart, beloveds, as I share the wisdom and blessedness of *"Valuing Relationships"* through personal and biblical experiences.

How does one value relationships?

Value: The regard that something is held to deserve, the importance, worth, or usefulness of something. A person's principle or standards of behavior; one's judgment of what is important in life.
-verb- Estimate the monetary worth of something. To value something or someone to be important or beneficial; have a high opinion of. To determine the worth or value of; appraise.

When valuing relationships, both people involved in a relationship will see how much they need one another. It takes both parties to see this instead of one. It takes two people to build a relationship, but one to tear it down.

In Romans 1:11-12, Apostle Paul spoke of how he longed to see the church in Rome to impart some spiritual gifts into them, and to be strengthen by their gifts.

Romans 1:11-12 (NLT): For I long to visit you so I can bring you some spiritual gift that will help you grow strong in the Lord. When we get together, I want to encourage you in your faith, but I also want to be encouraged by yours.

Many have lost this perception in relationships because they feel that they are strong enough or they alone came with something valuable to the table; thus implying that the other party involved is less important or doesn't have anything to offer to the relationship. This is pride **manifested.** When God connects you with someone, it's never for you to be a lone ranger, but for you to glean from that person as well. Teamwork is a MUST in relationships.

When one of the parties involved has gotten to a place where he or she feels elevated in his or her mind, and is at a place where they can't be taught nor receive anything from the other party, then the relationship has come to a time of separation. Jesus needed the 12 to fulfill, be strengthened, and be encouraged in His mission on this Earth. God, the Father, Himself needed the Son to fulfill His mission and give glory back to the Father. In the beginning, God said it was not good for man to be alone. So from the beginning, God saw how pride would mess up man, and He saw that man would need strength, encouragement and someone to share his life with. You can't be in a relationship if both parties aren't willing to build that relationship. You can't be intimate with someone who isn't intimate with you.

Malachi 4:5-6 speaks of the spirit of Elijah coming to turn the hearts of the fathers to the children, and the hearts of the children to the fathers.

This is relationship. This shows us that there's something of value in the children as well as the fathers, no matter how much more mature the fathers are than the children.

I have been told twice in my life, (that I can recall) that I have nothing that a person wants or needs from me. The first time I heard those words, I was hurt, but when I heard those words for the second time, they didn't bother me as much. **When someone says that you don't have anything to offer, please know that the person who spoke those words doesn't value their relationship with you or they don't see you as capable of giving them anything they need or want. Let the Holy Spirit use these situations to show you how to be flexible and show you how to bounce back like a palm tree.** Palm trees may bend out of shape a little, but they won't break. Personally, I've been known as a woman to love hard. I pursued and chased after people, even when they showed less interest in me than I showed to them. Though I may have been rejected and misunderstood, I still knew my value. I marked the palm tree because, even in relationships, things may AFFECT you but they don't have to INFECT you! You may be REJECTED but not suffer from the spirit of REJECTION.

Chapter 1
<u>Introducing "Real Love"</u>

1 John 4:9-10 (NLT) "God showed how much he loved us by sending his one and only Son into the world so that we have eternal life through him. This is REAL LOVE not that we loved God, but that he loved us, and sent his Son as a sacrifice to take away our sins."
1 John 4:19 (KJV) "We loved him, because he first loved us."

Many have went into relationships with the mentality of just wanting to receive love, but not wanting to give love in return. This is a dangerous pitfall. As people of God, we tend to have unrealistic expectations for others. We put demands on others that they are not equipped to fulfill. This type of desire will destroy many relationships because the root of bitterness rages against the love offered and deems it unfulfilling.

Introducing "Real Love"

For example: A wife who has never had a father figure in her life marries her husband with the expectation of him fulfilling some type of "fatherly love void". She is deeply disappointed because he can only successfully give her the love of a husband, but not the love of father.

So, our perception of love has been wrong. You see, we oftentimes go into relationships expecting to be repaired by love, but now is the time to refocus on the truth, and enter relationships with a "I want to give and show love" attitude. I know this will not be easy to do, and it may be torn down and not accepted, especially for those who are broken, but it can be done. 1 John 3:20 (NLT) says, Even if we feel guilty, God is greater than our feelings, and he knows everything.

<u>A Love Letter From Real Love</u>
(1 John 3:11-24, 4:7-21)

Dear My sons and daughters,

Introducing "Real Love"

From the very beginning was Love, and Love was with Me, and Love is Me. I created you, My habitation, and your existence in Love. I am Love, and all who want to be with Me must love Me with their whole being and show others Love as I have shown from the very beginning. Don't be like Cain who belonged to the evil one and killed his brother. Why did he kill him, you may ask? Cain had done what was evil, and his brother had done what was righteous. So don't be surprised, dear sons and daughters, if the world hates you. Loving your brothers and sisters proves that you have passed from death to life, but if you don't love your brothers and sisters, it shows Me that you are still dead. Anyone who hates his brothers and sisters is really a murderer at heart. You know that murderers don't have eternal life within them. Know what Real Love is, because I, Jesus, gave up My life for you. So you also ought to give up your lives for your brothers and sisters. If someone has enough money to live well and sees a brother or sister in need, but shows no compassion how can My Love be in them? Do not merely say that you love each other, but show that you belong to the truth, and this will give you confidence when you stand before Me. Even if you feel guilty, I, Love, am greater than your feelings, and I know everything. If you don't feel guilty, you can come to Me with bold confidence. In that time, you will receive from Me whatever you ask, because you obeyed Me and done the things that pleased Me. Believe in Me, and love one another; this is what I require of you. Obey these requirements and I will remain in fellowship with you. Oh, I would say again, sons and daughters, continue to love one another, for love comes from Me. Anyone who loves is My child and knows Me. Anyone who does not love, does not know Me, for I am Love. I showed you how much I loved you by sending My Son into the world so that you might have eternal life. This is real Love, not that you loved Me, but that I loved you and sent My Son as a sacrifice to take away your sins. Since, I loved you that much, you surely ought to love each other. No one has ever seen Me. If you love each other, I live in you, and My love is brought to full expression in you. I have given you My Spirit as proof that I live in you, and you in Me. All who confess that Jesus is the Son of God have Me living in them, and they in Me. Know how much I love you, so put your trust in Me. Remember, I, God, am Love, and all who live in love live in Me, and I live in them. As you live in Me, your love grows more perfect. So be not afraid on the day of judgment, but be confident, because you lived like Jesus Christ while here in this world. Love has no fear, because perfect love expels all fear. If you are afraid, it is for fear of punishment, and this shows that you have not fully experienced My perfect Love. Love each other as I have said before, because I loved you first. If someone says, "I love God," but hates his brother or sister, that person is a liar, for if you don't love the people you can see everyday, how can you love Me, whom you cannot see? So, My sons and daughters, please pursue Me with

Introducing "Real Love"

your whole heart, mind, soul and strength, and I'll take you places you have never been before. I love you.

Sincerely,
Real Love

Chapter 2
Rejected Love

When I was five years old, I felt pressured by my mom and aunts to tell the social workers that my dad molested me because of how my mom found me in the bed one night. It was on the night my mom left my sister, brother, and I in my dad's care while she when out. This interrupted my life and relationship with my dad. This situation caused my dad to become angry and neglect me. I was left confused, hurt and torn because I was uncertain of everything that happened on that night. So, my siblings and I were taken away from our parents to be put into a foster home, but my grandmother begged the social workers to put us into her care, and they did.

At first, living in a three bedroom house with four separate families was very hard to deal with. My grandmother did the best she could to raise all the families on her own. At this time,

Rejected Love

my uncle, my mom, and my aunt were addicted to drugs and alcohol, while my oldest brother sold drugs. Living in my grandmother's house was very hard because fights use to break out often.

At this time in my life, being between the ages of six to ten years old, elementary school had became difficult for me. I was picked on by boys everyday because my mom was on drugs, especially in the first grade. One day, I became so angry at them that I took my aggression and anger out on my teacher. I felt she was picking on me, so I kicked and threw a chair at her. This act resulted in me getting suspended, retained to the first grade, placed in speech class, and eventually placed in special education/behavioral classes. When they told me that they were going to put me in special education, I became very upset. I inquired about their reason for placing me in special education, and they said that I wasn't going because of my IQ, I was going because of my bad behavior. They said the class would be a class where special education and students with behavioral issues were taught together. Being in this class really didn't help my reputation with the boys; it actually made it worst. So, I had to look for ways to fit in with them and be loved by them. I found the popular, pretty girls and the girls who were known to beat up others and I began to bully some of them to gain a reputation with the popular boys. I picked fights with boys and girls regularly to try to fit in with the crowd.

During this stage of my life, I experienced so many visions, dreams and visitations. One night, when I was eight years old, my sister and I were in our beds sleeping when I began to get attacked by a demon. I woke up fighting as if I were fighting in the natural. This demon terrified me for most of the night until my grandmother heard me screaming. She came and got me out of my room and then took me into her bedroom. When we got into her bedroom, she poured holy oil and water into a wash pan, wiped me down from head to toe, anointed my body with holy oil, and then rebuked the devil off my life. She prayed over me, prophesied over me, spoke life into me and told me I was chosen by God. That night, my grandmother taught me about the fear of the Lord. She imparted so much of the Word of the Lord into me and she let me slept in her room with her. I fell asleep watching her lamp-stand burn. In her room, I felt safe because I knew the presence of the Lord was there. This was the beginning of my journey with the Lord.

After this encounter, I was so hungry to know about Jesus for myself. I heard the wisdom that Grandma and our pastor would share with us, but I knew there was more that I didn't know. I gave my life to Christ and began to excel in the things of the Lord very quickly. I was always a quick learner, and between the ages of eight and ten years old, I faithfully studied the bible. Within a month, I'd learned every book of the bible. My visions, dreams and visitations by angels increased, but I didn't understand them. My grandmother and pastors couldn't really tell me exactly what they meant other than I had a great calling on my life and encourage me stay obedient to the Lord. I

Rejected Love

began to understand more about casting out demons and the fear of the Lord as I assisted in working the altar with the adults as they cast out demons. I tarried for the Holy Ghost, helped assist with ministerial duties and showed others how to tarry for the Holy Ghost. At the age of ten, I became a youth leader, and I was placed over a section of the children's ministry. I was also over the youth choir and I became a Sunday school teacher. Although I was still in special classes for behavior and speech, my hunger for God meant more to me than my reputation with the kids at my school. I felt so much love at church that I didn't care about my reputation at school as much as I once did.

One day, a new family came into the church and we found out that we were relatives. At that time, I was eleven years old and in the fifth grade. One of the girls' name was Love. She quickly became my best friend. She also became an assistant with me in the youth choir. We were both loving on the Lord at that time; that was until my pastor's wife died and he remarried. His new wife had a 16 year old son who became a musician and a youth leader at our church. His older sister became the head youth leader and she also became a close friend of mines.

One day, our church celebrated its anniversary. By this time, I was 12 years old and in the sixth grade. My pastor's stepson and I were told to go and get some things out the house. While we were in the house, he asked me if I wanted to take a quick keyboard lesson and rehearse the song we were going to sing that following Sunday and I said yes. As I sat on the stool in front of the keyboard, he came closer to me. Suddenly, he grabbed my wrist, tried to kiss me and started to tell me that he'd always wanted me. I tried to get to the door to go back outside, but he grabbed me and threw me on the sofa. I struggled to get loose from him, but he was determined to rape me. I was wearing a dress, and of course, he'd lifted up my dress and tried to take my undergarments off. I broke away from him by kicking him in his genitals. I then ran out the house, and told the adults what he'd done. When I told the pastor and the pastor's wife, they rebuked and blamed me! This hurt me to the core of my heart, especially since my grandmother didn't stand up for me in front of the pastors. My would-be-rapist's sister, on the other hand, believed me because he had confided in her that he had a crush on me. I was angry with my grandmother because she hadn't protected or defended me, so I reverted back to my old habits. Once again, I began to fight a lot, I became rebellious, and I looked for validation anywhere I thought I could find it. I stop letting my grandmother style my hair, and I began to do my own hair. My oldest brother and I use to argue and fight often, and after he went to prison, I became very tom-boyish and very athletic. I became very involved in sports, and during this time, I bullied people extremely. I was also molested by an uncle, older cousins, uncles-in-laws, coaches, and flirted with by teachers. My mother and father considered reconciling with one another, and even though they'd successfully gotten back together at one time, they fought too much, so their relationship was short-lived. They continued to have an on-again, off-again relationship with one another.

At the age of 13, I'd lost my virginity and became sexually active. I looked for love in all the wrong places. I was solicited for sex with money and food by my uncles-in-law and coaches. They would either ask to touch me inappropriately or to have sex with me, and this continued until I told my grandma and aunts what they had been doing. I was confronted by the majority of my aunts at once, but once again, no one believed me, so they slandered me badly. My grandmother stood by and comforted me, telling me that my mother had gone through the very same ordeal. Growing up as a teenager wasn't easy, but I survived.

During this time in my life, I was raped, molested, prostituted, and physically abused. I was even left for dead many times lying on the road during a thunderstorm, on a bus, in condemned houses and so on. I ended up getting a steady boyfriend who I thought was

going to protect me, but he ended up physically abusing me. On one occasion, he'd beaten me so badly that I ended up having a miscarriage. Even after the death of my baby, I remained in a relationship with my baby's killer because I believed that he was the only person in this world who truly loved me, despite his jealous ways. He accepted me as I was, and he'd rescued me from some people who were trying to take advantage of me on one occasion, so I felt like I owed him my life. During this time in our relationship, my grandmother was getting older and had lost a leg. She still tried to maintain two growing families by herself, but it became too much of a burden for her to bear. There wasn't enough food for all of us anymore, so I began prostituting my body to my boyfriend so that I could help feed my sister, cousins and younger brother.
Eventually, I got out of that relationship, moved to another city with a friend, and got into another relationship, only to be raped at gunpoint. My rapist held a gun to my head and placed the barrel of his gun in my mouth. As a teen, I had to grow up rather quickly. My life

was a repeating cycle of violence and chaos throughout my teenage and young adult years.

At the age of 19, I came back to the Lord. I thought church would be better than it was when I was younger, because I was more mature and now around people of God who were more knowledgeable about the things of God. I thought that I was safe and no one would ever hurt me again. I thought my church family would help me and accept me as I was, but things didn't go as I'd hoped and expected. Instead, at the age of 20, while in ministry, I went through mental, emotional, spiritual and verbal abuse. Leaders who were within the ministry that I was submitted to abused their authority by misusing me. I was dominated, manipulated, slandered, lied on, stolen from, and taken advantage of with my money and car. After losing the family home in a fire, I was accepted into one leader's home, and there, I was threatened and mistreated. One day, when I was sleeping on the head intercessor/seer prophetess sofa, God woke me up to hear a conversation about me on the

Rejected Love

telephone, but instructed me to keep my eyes closed and keep quiet until a certain time. I listened to her slander, scandalize and lie on me so badly that I couldn't listen to it anymore. I then got up and walked into her prayer room and prayed bitterly to the Lord. After I got up from prayer, I said nothing concerning what I had heard; I just went on as if it never happened. I still showed love to her, did as I was told and I departed from her house that following weekend. Nevertheless, I still remained under her mentor-ship.

The following week, while working at the daycare, I'd walked up on another conversation being held by some co-workers and the head intercessor/seer prophetess about me. I was coming back from my break when I walked up on their conversation. During my lunch, I'd been in the sanctuary in prayer and worship with the Lord, and I was returning from my break to relieve one of my co-workers for lunch. I remained quiet at the door, and after this incident, I continued treating them as if I hadn't heard a thing. I praised, worshipped, and prayed to the Lord while the kids slept during nap time. When the kids got up, I loved on the kids because they were my inspiration. I gave the head intercessor much time, grace, and space to repent of her vindictive ways, for not only slandering my name, but for slandering other intercessors as well, but she remained unrepentant. Finally, one day, I decided to tell the senior leader/apostle about the incidents. He told me that he'd been previously informed about her behavior numerous times, and she'd slandered many who were a part of the cell group. So he set up a meeting with her about her conduct, but it seemed as if she got worse after that meeting, persecuting the babes of the cell group and slandering me even more. She even started coming to the daycare to talk about me consistently. This behavior continued even after I'd confronted her. Finally, I went to the apostle to tell him that I was removing myself from the intercessor/prophet's group because of the head intercessor's controlling and manipulative ways. A month later, the head intercessor/seer prophetess and I reconciled, and loved on each other again, but I kept my distance.

I tried so hard to look for love in many people and through a series of relationships, but my love was rejected time and time again.

During my four years in this ministry, I couldn't leave when I wanted to, even in the midst of persecution. I was instructed by God to stay until my time was up, and after that, He would reveal to me the time in which I was to depart. I finally received permission to separate myself from that ministry in 2006 when God instructed me to relocate to Atlanta, Georgia. Before I moved, I went back and forth with the Lord because I felt the area He was instructing me to move into put me at risk. God began to confirm His instructions to me by giving me vivid dreams, visions, signs, angelic visitations, and through his prophets, but I still feared this move. I tried to bargain with God because of my living situation and limited finances. Who was going to take care my mom? Plus, I definitely didn't want to leave my church. Even though I'd been mistreated by the cell group leader, overall, I loved her and my church, and I thought I would never find another ministry like the one I was in. The more I battled with God about the move, the more I felt pushed to go forward. I began to make plans and set a timeline to move to Atlanta, but I kept hearing God tell me to leave. The more I kept seeking advice from others in ministry, the more I kept being pushed by God.

One day, I went to meet with my Pastor/Apostle and tell him about the instructions God had given me in reference to relocating. I wanted his permission, blessing and counsel. In our meeting, he asked me to demonstrate to him how God had given those instructions to me, where I was being instructed to move to, and confirmation of the directions. I kept records of my visions in my journal, and that included any prophecies I'd received. He then said to me, "I love you and don't want you to go, but if you feel that God has instructed you to go, I give you my blessing to go forward." A few weeks later, I was still trying to get permission from others about the move until one day while I was in prayer, God sternly asked me, "Why are you still getting permission from others when you have already gotten permission from me?"

The Cost of Disobedience

During my last weeks working at the daycare, God began to warn me about some impending events that would occur. One day, me and two of my friends made plans to go to a gospel concert and service at Bishop Eddie Long's church that upcoming weekend. The church was in Lithonia, Georgia. One night, I dreamed of my house burning down. Then, another night, God woke me up and told me to go into my den. When I went into the den, the firewood was outside of the fireplace burning on the carpet right beside the sofa. I looked in amazement at the firewood burning on the carpet because it didn't blaze up. I then went into the living room and saw my oldest brother drunk and asleep on the sofa, while my mom was in her room asleep. I woke everyone up to tell them what I'd witnessed and I showed them the burn marks on the floor. The next day, I went to stay with my friend because we were preparing to go to Atlanta. The following morning, I went home and packed my bags. When I arrived at the house, my mom blew the horn to warn my brother that I was coming because he was in my room. I told my mom that I would return home that following Sunday.

My friends and I were in Atlanta doing a little shopping before church service, when they realized that they had a lot of missed calls. We went to a quiet area in the mall so that they could check their phones, but their phones began to ring. They were both receiving calls from some of their friends telling them that my house had just burned down. We all thought that they were joking until one of my friends received a phone call from one of the church members. She happened to be visiting the city that I lived in and she had never been to my house. She told me that my house was on fire and she was watching it burn as we spoke. My room was the only room in the house with the door closed, but the fire burned every other

Rejected Love

room in the house except my room. The church member who'd witnessed the fire later told me that she'd spoken with a few people, and they'd all said it was evident who was praying in that house because my room hadn't been touched by the fire. I found out that my oldest brother was asleep on the same sofa I'd seen him drunk on days earlier. He ended up having to go to the hospital because he had a lot of smoke in his lungs, but thank God, he was okay. This tragic event immediately reminded me of the warnings God had given me that previous week. Instead of returning home, we decided to stay in Atlanta, because there was nothing I could do, nor was there anything that I needed to go back for.

After service, I felt lost because I didn't know what I was going to do. My mother and I were homeless again. Many people said they would be there for us, but they weren't. We sought help everywhere.
One night, my mom and I were about to sleep in my car in a motel parking lot, but by the grace of God, a young lady who worked at the

motel came up to my car and gave us a room to stay in. None of our friends or family would accept my mom into their homes, but I knew that I had to take care of her. I refused to go into any one's home who wouldn't accept my mother. That following weekend, we went to the church to ask for help, and they finally wrote us a small check that allowed us to get into an apartment for three days. We didn't have enough for any utilities, so we didn't have lights, water, or heat. We only had a mattress. I felt rejected by everyone again, and I felt the very ones who'd said they would be there for us had abandoned us.

Travailing
On February 14, 2006, one of our relatives allowed my mother stay with them. That night, I stayed alone in the cold apartment and cried bitterly before the Lord. I wanted to know why I was going through what I was going through, but the only thing God showed me was a vision of a pair of pants. The pants had a pocket with a heart on it, and within the heart, I saw the word 'PUSH'. The next day, I woke up early

that morning, picked my mom up and we went to Atlanta to look for an apartment. As we were getting closer to the city, I received a call from my aunt's best friend. She told me about some apartments that her daughter lived in, and she gave me her daughter's phone number. I called her daughter and she told me about the apartments. So, my mother and I went to Stone Mountain, Georgia to apply for those apartments. I received favor from the Lord. He gave us the miracle that we needed. We were able to get into the apartment we'd applied for with no money down. I couldn't be mad at anyone but myself because of disobedience, even though everything eventually worked out for my good.

You see, I looked for love from everyone, even felt abandoned by God and others, but the whole time I needed to put my trust and confidence in God alone to take care of me and fill the voids that were in my life and heart.

Chapter 3
<u>Exploring New Heights of God's Love</u>

The First Love Commandments:
<u>Loving God with all my heart, all my soul, all my mind, and all my strength.</u>
Mark 12:29-34, Jesus replied, "The most important commandment is this: Listen, O Israel! The Lord our God is the one and only Lord. And you must love the Lord your God with all your heart, all your soul, all your mind, and all your strength."

It was a week that our Apostle (my husband) had been teaching on deliverance, and the ministry was being purged from its impurities. You see, when you began to teach on deliverance, demons began to manifest severely because of their operations, strategies, assignments, and works are being exposed. In this time of exposure, demons still don't want to leave the vessels, so they began to manifest themselves in the people in your life. People began to get uncomfortable and shaken up around you. So, you will have to ask the Lord to help you manage and deal with such situations. In this week, I shut in with the Lord and shut out outside influences. I got delivered from myself and gave myself to God as a living sacrifice, holy and acceptable, which was my reasonable service. This process positioned me to be in place for God to show me my own heart. He revealed to me my next assignment, the state of the people in the ministry I was a part of, challenging situations that were to come, and He warned me about the plots of the enemy. This shut-in helped me to better guard my heart, discipline my will and emotions, pull down strongholds, and cast down imaginations and evil thoughts. It also renewed my mind, and gave me renewed strength.

During the shut-in, I had a three part dream. In this dream, I was getting persecuted; nevertheless, I still demonstrated love to the people who were persecuting me. Despite my efforts, the crowd grew and my faith weakened. Then, I was caught up in the sky by tons of feathers and wings. Eagles then began to soar on the backs of the feathers and wings. They took me to a city where I had to be trained. I was being trained by governors, policemen, firefighters and those who held high positions. They told me to walk first over the hurdles that I was facing, and then, run as fast as I could. They continued telling me not to give up when I was getting tired in my body and to keep going so I continued my laps in spite of all of the obstacles that were in my way. I passed that test, and I was assigned to show others how to exercise as I had done. So, I did.

The next day, I was hit hard by slander; unusual manifestations in people in the ministry began to happen, onslaughts by the spirit of Saul (former leadership) and financial mishaps, happened. My preparation caused me to be prepared for situations that were going to come any way. It caused me to stay in character even when everything else around me acted unseemly. You see this dream warned and strengthen me to press forward in spite of situations and circumstances. Now if I would have failed the test I would've continued going in circles. I came out with victory! "Glory to Our God for not giving up on me and revealing to redeem"!!!!

Loving God with all your heart...
Jeremiah17:9-10 NLT... The human heart is the most deceitful of all things, and desperately wicked. Who really knows how bad it is? But I, the Lord, search all hearts and examine secret motives. I give all people their due rewards, according to what their actions deserve."

Loving God with all your heart caused me to reposition my priorities. When we do this God will lead us. The word of God tells us in Proverbs 4:23 Guard our heart from all envy and strife. We must see that the heart is very fertile, easily to influenced, can be manipulated, can deceive and be deceived, can be vexed, desire to lead us, wants revenge and will demand its own way. Many say let your heart lead you, but I say don't let your heart lead you if your heart is not in alignment with God and His desires. As the scripture says the heart is desperately wicked who can know it but God. You don't really know your heart until you get put into a situation that will cause your heart to be tried, tested and revealed. This is the more reason why it is very important to guard your heart, because out it will flow the issues of life that will vent out strife, envy, malice and all types of evils. We have to train and discipline our own heart to seek God, love God, follow God, love God people and give away to God all it cares. God desire and will is to circumcise our old rugged heart and give us a new heart. God wants us to love like He love and pursue those things like He does.

In this week I began to give all my heart to my Lord and let him know how I felt in the midst of my situations. I told him I was tired of things in the same way and to create in me a clean heart and renew a right spirit within me. I told him to help me to guard my heart because I was tired of letting things in it that was causing me to be moved by people opinions and it was weighing heavy upon me. I was tired of going in circles with the same oh feelings and needing help. I didn't want to hold resentment in my heart and wanted to be free with a pure heart. You see I used to share lots of my heart with others that truly didn't value me instead of sharing it with God first. I was only giving my God now the leftovers instead my all. I didn't see him as my Alpha and Omega anymore (though my mouth was speaking it). My heart was sick, because I had giving my whole heart to everyone else besides God. These sickening times in my life caused me to return to my first love. I began to tell God how sorry I was. He reminded me about how we use to commune and be intimate with each other. He returned me to my love letters to him, where I use to give my whole heart to him. As I would write my letters to Him, I would sing it to him, which would bring deliverance, healing and freedom. I now had began to see that He is my only secret keeper, who to be completely transparent with. He was the one to whom I give all my heart too without thinking he will betray me or give away my secrets to use against me. So I urge you to give all your heart to God.

Many times people will try to say God knows my heart as an excuse to do wrong, but have you truly gave God your heart? Have you given God the secret motives of your heart? Have you given God your true heart desires? Have you giving God the jealousy of heart? Have you truly given God your offenses, hurts, anger, resentment, and bitterness? I feel if we would truly give God all our hearts, our hearts will be in better shapes. Our hearts will seek after the things of God. Our hearts will truly forgive others when they wrong us. Our hearts will line up with the heart desires of the heart of God. Our walk and actions will line up with Obedience to His will.

My Journey of the Lover of My Heart

During the years of 2008 through 2010, I was challenged by all types of persecution from every angle. I was being persecuted badly by peers, family, friends, in-laws, church members and leaders, that abused, used, mistreated me, betrayed and slandered me. I was oppressed hard by serving under head leadership with the spirit of Saul, to where it even interrupted and affected my marriage. Every angle I was getting attacked and tried, that it caused me to have a nervous breakdown. Being in ministry at my local church was very difficult for me to cope with but I had to constantly rely on God to keep me in the mist of it all. I looked at it as another stage of my training and development. I remain faithful and loyal to my leaders and husband knowing God was shifting us all. I submitted to and patiently waited on my husband training even-though it was extremely difficult. Being in a small town, getting new friends wasn't easy as well, because when others find out who I was friends with, they began to tell all types of negativity about me to taint and distort the new friend perception of me that tore our relationship. Being in ministry that caused me much harm, where I really didn't have no choice to be in at the time, because my husband was a member there, where we both serve faithfully together and separately in leadership. I had no other choice but to submit my heart and will to the process. God allowed me to be stripped and torn down all the way until there wasn't really nothing left of me. All had forsaken me locally and I was left standing alone with my God wailing and travailing for a way out. These were even more times I had to really learn how to give my whole heart to God and not to put all my trust in man alone. Everyone was coming up short every time. Serving in this ministry even in leadership caused me to start a journey of the Lover of my heart.

God had to really cause a circumcision to my heart here. I became so numb to the pain of rejection and persecution because of the repetition of it. However, in all of this, I still remained faithful to my assignments in the ministry and learned to show love to them despite who they were. I would just say they know not what they do and if they do I still forgive them. When I would see these same cycles occur I would say here goes it again with the same ones that say they value our relationship. It had become so bad in ministry there of how some would treat me, that when I would go up to the leaders and colleagues in the ministry that was trying to withdraw from me, those that scandalized my name, those that tried to assassinate my character, those that resented me, and plot in the hearts about me, I would then run after them to give them a huge hug, a kiss on the cheek, encouraging and kinds words. I showed as much love as I could when they would do this but they still would, turn their nose up at me and be rude. I would be appalled and giggle within, seeing how some leaders even the senior leader would literally run from me to avoid speaking to me. However, in my different approach of this, I controlled my heart, inspite of what it felt like it wanted to do.

These were times when I felt like God would instigate something and harden their hearts toward me, to cause an occasion to happen to drive me back to Him, because I was getting too comfortable with a person and didn't value me and His relationship as I said I did. God knows I'm a loyal person that loves hard and when I say I'm with you, I am. During these times in my life, I would always hear God call me "Daughter of Zion" that would melt my heart to pieces like a little girl. I would come to Him as a little girl comes to her natural father. I used to paint this mental picture of me coming to Daddy God as I used to call Him, then sit on His lap and tell Him All my cares because I knew He cared for me. He would love those times as I did this too. He would reveal so much of Himself and hidden plots to me, which included, the revealing plots of the enemies. He would touch my heart with His gentle and comforting words that strengthen my whole being, to be strong, courageous and of an encourage heart. He would sing songs to me and over me through different expressions of His love. He would prophesy to me life-giving and changing words. He would let me know He would never leave me, nor forsake me. He would let me know that I wasn't insane, crazy or what other names others would try to label me as. These times were so humbling yet soothing because I would go through it hard among others but would get loved on so dearly alone by God that it didn't matter what happened that they had done that day or time to me. My God, them were the times. Times like this would cause you to really appreciate your long-sufferings. Who say that a nation can't be birth in one day! I'm a living testimony! Hallelujah!

Loving God with all your Mind...
Philippians 4:8, And now, dear brothers and sisters, one final thing. Fix your thoughts on what is true, honorable, right, pure, lovely, and admirable. Think about things that are excellent and worthy of praise.

We ask ourselves, how do we love God with all our mind? Apostle Paul tells us to think on those things that are pure, honorable, right, lovely, just and holy. He shows us how to exercise discipline in our thought patterns. We see that this truly will take discipline and time to develop, but it can be done. This is why we always need to return to our first love with God, because it will keep our minds renewed. God always gives us a mental picture of His love so we could expound on His beauty and all His majesty. Such things give us a hope, future and an expectant end. This is my daily exercise in discipline my thought life and it should be yours as well. As the heart gets purified the mind began to line up better to focus on the things of God. Watch what you give your attention to and stay out of unquestionable thinking. Guard your gates, because it will feed curiosity, which we see, what happened to Eve from the beginning.

Truly the mind is a battlefield and we have to discipline our thoughts daily. Satan tries to throw things such as doubts and fears to us by causing us to doubt the one that we suppose to give our minds to. We have to train our thoughts to think on the pure, holy things, and things of good report. So when those negative thoughts try to arise. We immediately cast those thoughts down, giving your mind to God that cause you to have the sound mind of Christ.

Exploring New Heights of God's Love

I remember the time when everyone that said they will be there for me left me, and persecuted me. So when this happened, I began to examine myself but when examining myself, I began to entertain negative condemning thoughts. These thoughts caused me to have a nervous breakdown, to where I attempted to run away and even contemplate committing suicide. Satan seize this vulnerable and rejected time in my life, used it as his playground, until I came to myself, took control of my thought life and gave my mind to Christ. I started to think of those precious moments I spent with God, the promises God had spoken over my life. The instructions He had given to me, that cause me to walk in obedience to Him.

There will be times when the thoughts of your carnal mind will try to come rationalize the plans and thoughts of God but we have to resist these thoughts and embrace the sound mind of Christ Jesus. I can recall a time in my life in ministry when the enemy would come to paralyze my mind with the fear of the crowd while I was up preaching, teaching or leading praise and worship until God sent a prophetess of God to my house to advise me as what to do when I'm up leading God people in worship. She told me that I have the Love, I have the power but for my sake it now times to call forth the sound mind of Christ Jesus being in the mist of the crowd. I thanked God for this woman of God that brought this word of wisdom to me, that has changed my life which brought a more excellent way to me for ministry. For truly a carnal mind is an enemy of God.

Loving God with all your soul...
The Journey of Forgiveness
Psalm 37:4 NLT...Take delight in the Lord, and he will give you your heart's desires.

Loving God with all your soul is to love him with all your emotions, will, mind, agenda, motive and desires. The Lord says if you remain in me and my word in you, I will give you your heart desires. It also tells us to seek first the kingdom of God; His righteousness and all these things will be added. You have to make the Lord the Lover of your Soul. You have to take delight in the Lord. You have to deny and submit your will for His will and say nevertheless, not as I will but your will be done. You would have to long for Him as you would your spouse but much more. Remember you're His bride too. Find out His likes and dislikes. Find out what pleases Him. Get to know Him again. Once you began to make Him your all and all, you'll become one with Him then what He desire will become your desires, what He hates will become your hate and who become your enemies will be His enemies. Lavish your love on Him and long for Him all the day long.

Do you remember when you first felled in love with your spouse? He would be right beside you whispering those sweet nothings to you or you guys would be traveling together in the same car but you still want to be even closer to him the more as if he's not with you where you would feel like you miss him, feeling like he was far away. That's how you should feel about our God, but more. Jesus presence is so refreshing and ravishing. Guys I could stay in this realm all day long, because my whole-being loves being saturated by His love. Ahhhh!!! Oh, How I love me some HIM!!!

I remember when I began a journey of forgiveness. I wrote down and collected all the people that I was holding bondage in my heart and soul that I had to forgive. This journey wasn't easy but I pressed and forgave. My will said no but I said God your will for me is to let go and that's what I did.

I named this journey, "My journey of forgiveness"...
On this journey I received a level of freedom like never before. I examined my life and heart, and then asked Holy Spirit to expose to me who I was holding captive in my heart and soul. Then He began to reveal. In this revealing process, it brought a shock to me. The reason of the shock is because I thought I had forgiving certain ones but come to find out that the heart has deceitfully deceived me and I didn't know it. So when I thought I had

forgiving, I come to find out that I truly haven't. On the contrary, it was just that they haven't been not around and I had suppressed it. So I came to grips that I had to forgive and release people out of my spirit, letting them go so I can move on to destiny. In pursuing Christ Jesus, it will always reveals the hidden kept secrets and issues of our hearts, soul, will and motives, which will lead us on to perfection. In His word it says the ones that bear fruit, He prunes to bears much more fruit. He Jesus is coming back for a church without spot, blemish, or wrinkles.

Understanding forgiveness through the eyes of Love is an understanding that's beyond our feelings. When we choose to love someone it's beyond the way they love you or if they choose to love you in return. Forgiving others is beyond the way you feel when you say you're forgiving someone. It's taking the necessary steps in forgiving someone. So when you do this and your feelings try to come to condemn you, you remember that Real True Love is greater than our heart feelings and desires. We then take on the desires of God love that's unconditional that requires us to love beyond. I want to hear those words from the Lord that says Well Done Good and Faithful servant for you learned to Love. He is good so that makes me good too. When God looked at all His creation in the book of Genesis He called it good but when HE was finished with creating man and woman He then said it was VERY good. Well some of you may say that Jesus said there was none good except the Father. Perhaps Jesus said this because of the sinful desires in this mortal body, but when He died and resurrected Him then was transformed into His Glorious Perfect immortal body as it was with Adam from the beginning before the falling of mankind when God said it was VERY good. As it was in the beginning before the fall of mankind in the immortal bodies, so will it be again and oh will the Heavenly Father rejoice in His heart and say it again it is VERY GOOD being proud and pleased with Himself and all His accomplishments. WOW, what a time it will be!

Exploring New Heights of God's Love

When we get to the place, that place that says I will Love God with all my heart, all my soul, all my mind and all my strength it will truly mean, I will love unconditionally inspite of how I feel or how someone else treats me. It' also will be a sacrificial love. It's a place where others won't love you in return but it won't stop you from loving them. It's a place when others will spitefully misuse, abuse, mistreat, and curse you but you still will love them in return. I perceive that Love and forgiveness is a requirement by God. For this is the only way you will see God clearly then be forgiving and accepted by Him. In our demonstration of Love we must become patient with ourselves because fear and condemnation will try to overcome, overthrow and consume the love within us but we must continue to exercise love ourselves to be able to mature in and master love. Love yourself! You will have to begin practicing loving yourself and others, being your own coach and mentor in mastering demonstrated love. You will have to perfect love until love is perfected within you. In your coaching yourself and practicing love, you will then notice your improvement by saying I am learning how to love until you come to that point that says I did learn how to love. As you master one level of love, you then will go to a higher place in exploring different languages of love, to learn how to love on and in that place. In that mastering place of learning to love, you then will come to the place of mastering it until love has become the master over you, to whereas now you are led by God's true love. So remember, love and forgiveness is more than just an emotional feeling, it's a requirement but one must make the choice of choosing to behave in a loving way.

Loving God with all your strength...
Isaiah 40:29-31NLT... He gives power to the weak and strength to the powerless. Even youths will become weak and tired, and young men will fall in exhaustion. But those who trust in the Lord will find new strength. They will soar high on wings like eagles. They will run and not grow weary. They will walk and not faint.

We must learn to trust God with all that we have no matter what. Every day of our lives we're face with challenging situations and sometimes these situations weakens our faith, but we must continue to remain strong in the Lord. Lots of times, we depend upon our own understanding, gifts, and in our own ability to do things but if we continue to do this, we will remain defeated. Holy Spirit is what our God has giving us, to strengthen us in times of need. Let's take a look at the great examples of other great men of God as they were too thrust to do the Lord's work and needed His strength to sustain them.

Jeremiah16:19-21 NLT... Lord, you are my strength and fortress, my refuge in the day of trouble! Nations from around the world will come to you and say, "Our ancestors left us a foolish heritage, for they worshipped worthless idols. Can people make their own gods? These are not real gods at all!" The Lords says, "Now I will show them my power; now I will show them my might. At last they will know and understand that I am the Lord.

Exploring New Heights of God's Love

Jeremiah 17:5 NLT... This is what the Lord says: "Cursed are those who put their trust in mere humans, who rely on humans strength and turn hearts away from the Lord.

Acts 1:8 NLT... But you will receive power when the Holy Spirit comes upon you. And you will be my witnesses, telling people about me everywhere in Jerusalem, throughout Judea, in Samaria, and to the ends of the earth.

2 Corinthians 12:9-10 NKJV... And he said to me, "My grace is sufficient for you, for My strength is made perfect in weakness" Therefore most gladly I will rather boast in my infirmities, that the power of Christ may rest upon me. Therefore I take pleasure in infirmities, in reproaches, in needs, in persecution, in distresses, for Christ's sake. For when I am weak, then I am strong.

Many of you probably can testify about the times when it got to hard and difficult for you on this journey. You came to a place where you became battle fatigue because of the trials, storms, persecutions and tribulations to a point you wanted to give up and throw in the towel but you cried out for strength and our Lord came in, bore you up upon His shoulders and then strengthen you to continue the race. Reminding you that the race is not given to swift or the strong but to the one that endures to the end.

Chapter 4
The Second Love Commandment: "Love your Neighbor As Yourself"

Luke 10:29-37 NLT...The man wanted to justify his actions, so he asked Jesus, "And who is my neighbor?" Jesus replied with a story: "A Jewish man was traveling from Jerusalem down to Jericho, and he was attacked by bandits. They stripped him of his clothes, beat him up, and left him half dead beside the road. By chance a priest came by along. But when he saw the man lying there, he crossed to the other side of the road and passed him by. A Temple assistant walked over and looked at him lying there, but he also passed by the other side. Then a despised Samaritan came along and when he saw the man, he felt compassion for him. Going over to him, the Samaritan soothed his wounds with olive oil and wine and bandaged them. Then he put the man on his own donkey and took

The Second Love Commandment

him to an inn, where he took care of him. The next day he handed the innkeeper two silver coins, telling him, Take care of this man. If his bill runs higher than this, I'll pay you the next time I'm here. Now which of these three would you say was your neighbor to the man who was attacked by bandits? Jesus asked? The man replied, "The one who showed him mercy." Then Jesus said, "Yes, now go and do the same.

There are times in our lives in the local church, where robbery of your identity happens. The anointing on your life prostituted. Your gifts and callings get used up and abused for others own selfish gain. You're taken advantage of, then threaten, controlled, manipulated, mistreated, slandered and persecuted so badly you because you now refuse to stay and take more. Although, these things happen in churches, they're not limited there. You will also see them happening in several of relationships such as marriages, friendships, courtships, families, on jobs and so on. You can see by now that it happened to me in my

The Second Love Commandment

life and I know you probably can testify of having similar testimonies.

Here in these passages of scriptures, our Lord is showing us how to demonstrate his love toward our neighbor. We also see that the Religious, Prideful, Selfish and inconsiderate people (leaders in particular) that didn't care to help this Jewish man that was stripped, beat and robbed, just walked pass him as if seeing a stray hurt dog on the side of the road. When God sees His people in such a state as this, He will send love to deliver and restore them. He will send modern-day Samaritans people that will come to help heal and bind up the broken-heartedness. He will send people to show others how to love and receive love again. He will send burden-bearers that will shoulder burdens of others as if it was their own. In this state God longs to see us made free again.

Isaiah 61 NLT... The "Spirit of the Lord God is upon me, for the Lord has anointed me to bring good news to the poor: He has sent me to comfort the brokenhearted, and to proclaim that captives will be released, and prisoner will be freed. He has sent me to tell those who mourn that the time of the Lord's favor have come, and with it, the day of Godly anger against their enemies. To all who mourn in Israel, he will give a crown of beauty for ashes, a joyous blessing instead of mourning, festive praise instead of despair. In their righteousness, they will be like great oaks that the Lord has planted for his own glory.

God longs for us His people to illustrate Isaiah 61. Being in relationships where there is no value, you will tend to see many robberies. Where there is no value, there is robbery. The ministry that God gave me my husband is truly of ministry of reconciliation. Our ministry was already functioning before it was named as House of Refuge. For truly our houses was known as the house of refuge. Many would come to escape danger and harm. Many would come that was broken, bruised and battered. Many would come to transition to another location. My husband and I would take homeless people in our houses to stay until they get situated.

I can recall a time when I was going to GED school, where I met this woman I never knew. God began to show me this woman life and all she had went through. He showed me how she was broken and was stripped in ministry to where she needed healing and deliverance. While we were on break in school, we all waited out in the hallway until time to go inside. So there I began to hear this woman talking to another woman. I can tell she was broken and speaking out of a place of bitterness and hurt. As I continued to listen to her even impart error and rebellion into the babe in Christ, I prayed within and asked Holy Spirit when was the time to interject. He instructed me to listen a little further and so I did. Then He spoke and said it was time and I did. I corrected this woman in love. She looked at me like, who do you think you are. As I spoke her she said but in rebuttal but I continued and it pierced her heart that she couldn't say nothing else but agree, wail up with tears in her eyes and said to me you must be Seer Prophetess. I smiled and said I'm just a messenger from the Lord to help restore His people and return them back to His love. The other woman which was a babe thanked me and tried to give me praise but I redirected it back unto God. I embraced both of the women with a hug, and then the time came to where we all had to go back in class. At this time my teacher said she was going to put the class in groups because of what she was about assign us to do. She put me with the woman of God I corrected in love to where it was just us. This woman of God shared so much of her life to me as what God had already shown me and what I had touched on a little when I corrected her. She began to show me her prophet books she had with her and said she was a Seer Prophetess. In her testifying the more she mentioned to me her living situation and I was moved with compassion to invite her and her 2 kids to stay with us but I would call her to confirm it to her later that day after discussing it with my husband. This woman of God had just moved from South Carolina a day before I met her. When I discussed it with my husband we

The Second Love Commandment

decided to take this family into our home. I called her and said that we were coming to pick them up. We ministered healing, deliverance, love and provided for this family until they found a place. Many called me crazy for doing this as I understood them but I too remembered how it felt in a situation like that.

We took many into our homes as I've said and still to this day we do the same but we have gained more wisdom over the years because of being taken advantage of and disrespected in our own home. The moral of my story is to remember the 2nd commandment of Love and to love your neighbor as yourself. God is a God of relationships and He sent His son to reconcile us back to Him when He also was treated in a like manner. Remember yourself in this case, be wise in your actions and decisions and be moved with compassion seeing your neighbor like this. God is married to the backslider. God calls home the prodigals and we must welcome this with outstretched arms. The people that God has sent to our old house to live were prodigal's sons and

The Second Love Commandment

daughters. They were in relationships that caused them to be in the same state as the Jewish man that got robbed by bandits.

I pray your life begins to reflect the wisdom and love of the Lord to move with compassion when you see others in need deliverance. Don't be like the leaders that looked over the Jewish man and walked on by him. Restore your brother and sister to health, loving and treating as you would your own self. Let your life and dwelling place become a safe haven to them in their transitioning and recovery place. As the name of our ministry and logo name on our banner began to become your presence as well. I pray your presence and dwelling place become "The House of Refuge a place of safety and safe havens for kingdom building".

Chapter 5
Covenant People Versus Divine Connections

Covenant People can go on with their individual lives, separate for a time but still find themselves back with one another as if they were talking yesterday. Covenant people create bonds that say: "Your people are my people. Your enemies are my enemies". Covenant people are people that make a long lasting even lifetime promise or agreement to always be there for you. These are the people that will have your back no matter what. People that show unconditional love and support no matter how far you go. Even if you disagree about a matter or even if you abandon or stray away, they are still there for you as they remember and value the covenant that was made between you and them.

Divine Connection is people that are sent as well by God to only help you accomplish a particular assignment until their season and time is up.

Covenant is defined in the Webster as a binding agreement, a promise, and a contract, a pledge, usually formal, between two or more persons to do or not do something specified.

Divine is define in the Webster as relating to or coming from God or a god; deity. Extremely pleasant; delightful. Supremely good or beautiful. Relating to, or associated with. To perceive or understand something by inspiration or insight. To discern a hidden or future reality as though by supernatural power.

Connections is defined in the Webster as a relationship in which a person, thing, or idea is linked or associated with something else. The act of connecting. The state of being connected. An association or relationship.

It's powerful how God will use the ones that despise you to get you to the ones that will bless you. God will use the ones that will reject you to get you to the ones that are supposed to be divinely connected or in covenant with you.

Knowing the Seasonal Divine Connections Versus Longevity Covenant People.

When God send covenant people into your life you can guaranteed that there be with you a life time but when divine connections comes into your life it's to help you fulfill and accomplish a particular task until completed then it's time to move on. These divine connections can be people known as Mentors and Spiritual Midwives. They are considered divine connections because they are sent by God to you to accomplish and fulfill a particular assignment in your life in a particular season. Unlike covenant people such as Fathers, Mother, Brothers, Sisters and some Friends that God has sent to you that will be with you forever no matter what may come your way, how far you may go, where you may live or how long you may talk, they are still there.

It's imperative to know the difference of the relationship and its time span, so that you would know how to pour into and it's boundaries. Many have (myself included) in the past has gotten bent out of shape because someone left our life sooner than what we expected. They may have told you that y'all time were up but you insisted on trying to lengthen the timing and season of the relationship not knowing that it had ran its course.

Let's look at some relationships that was divinely connected and some that are longevity.

Titus And Paul Type Of Relationship
Paul and Titus relationship was shown as a longevity covenant people. Titus was a spiritual son of Apostle Paul and they kept their love, support and promise even until death. Titus 3:12-15

Titus 1:4 I am writing to Titus, my true son in the faith that we share. May God the Father and Christ Jesus our Savior give you grace and peace.

Paul And Timothy Type Of Relationship
Paul and Timothy relationship as well shown as a longevity covenant people. He too was a spiritual son of Apostle Paul.

1st Timothy 1:2 I am writing to Timothy, my true son in the faith. May God the Father and Christ Jesus our Lord give you grace, mercy, and peace.1 Timothy 6:11-21, 2 Timothy 4.

Barnabas And Paul Type Of Relationship
Barnabas and Paul was divinely connected and sent out to fulfill particular assignments until there appointed time came to disconnect.

Acts 9:26-27 When Saul arrived in Jerusalem, he tried to meet with the believers, but they were all afraid of him. They did not believe he had truly become a believer. Then Barnabas brought him to the apostles and told them how Saul had seen the Lord on the way to Damascus and how the Lord had spoken to Saul. He also told them that Saul had preached boldly in the name of Jesus in Damascus.

Covenant People Versus Divine Connections

Acts 13:2 One day as these men were worshipping the Lord and fasting, the Holy Spirit said, Dedicate Barnabas and Saul for the special work to which I have called them. So after more fasting and prayer, the men laid their hands on them and sent them on their way.

Acts 15:36-39 After some time Paul said to Barnabas, Let's go back and visit each city where we previously preached the word of the Lord, to see how the new believers are doing. Barnabas agreed and wanted to take along John Mark. But Paul disagreed strongly, since John Mark had deserted them in Pamphylia and had not continued with them in their work. Their disagreements were so sharp that they SEPARATED.

You see in the separation that Paul became so furious about John Mark going on the next journey with them. Paul understood value and comment. When he saw that John Mark no longer saw the value nor was true to his commitment, he knew it was the wise thing to not let him follow them. John Mark spoke with his lips about how he will be with them no matter what but when it came down to testing to see if he would he failed and didn't stay true to his commitment. Valuable lesson never take someone with you that don't truly value the relationship or the assignment as they say they do.

Paul And Silas Type Of Relationship
Silas and Paul as well was divinely connected and sent out to fulfill a specific assignment until the appointed time to their departure. Acts 9:26

Acts 16:40 Paul CHOSE Silas, and as he left, the believers entrusted him to the Lord's gracious care. Then he traveled throughout Syria and Cilicia, strengthening the churches there.

Acts 17:14 The believers acted at once, sending Paul on to the coast, while Silas and Timothy remained behind. Those escorting Paul went with him all the way to Athens, then they returned to Berea with instructions for Silas and Timothy to hurry and join him.

We see here as well that Silas and Timothy were divinely connected for a specific assignment in Berea.

Ruth And Naomi Type Of Relationship
Ruth and Naomi were shown as a longevity covenant people.

Ruth 1:14-19 And again they wept together, and Orpah kissed her mother-in-law good-bye. But Ruth clung tightly to Naomi. Look, Naomi said to her, your sister-in-law has gone back to her people and to her gods. You should do the same. But Ruth replied, Don't ask me to leave you and turn back. Wherever you go, I will go: wherever you live, I will live. Your people will be my people, and your God will be my God. Wherever you die, I will die, and there I will be buried. May the Lord punish me severely if I allow anything but death to separate us! When Naomi saw that Ruth was determined to go with her, she said nothing more. So the two of them continued their journey.

Ruth 4:15 May he restore your youth and care for you in your old age. For he is the son of your daughter-in-law who loves you and has been better to you than seven sons!

Spiritual Midwives

Spiritual midwives are shown as divine connectors that are there to help assist the parent in their time of preparation, delivery and afterbirth by cultivating, developing, instructing, and teaching them how to get prepared for conception. They are there to show how to adjust to the shifts, how to endure the pressures, how to stand firm in the mist of the transition and how to hold on in the time of hard labor pangs and contractions of the stages of pregnancy. They are there to show how to get prepared for delivery and birth. They are there to show how to nurture, mold and shape a healthy baby. Spiritual midwives are seasonal as a resembling of mentors. However, there are spiritual midwives that are spiritual parents as well as spiritual midwives but not all spiritual midwives are spiritual parents.

Examples; Sarah to Hagar, Moses Mom Yocheved (which was Puah), Moses sister Miriam (which was Shiphrah), Moses wife Tziporah, Asher, Hebrew women (Exodus 1:17-21), Deborah, An angel of the Lord to Samson mother and father Manoah, Mary and Elizabeth, Priest Eli to Samuel, Joseph to Mary, Titus 2:4 instructed the older women, Paul to the Romans. Just to name a few.

*Puah means to beautify, and/or to swaddle and clean baby.
*Shiphrah means cry, coo or groan because of the way she soothed and cooed the crying newborn infants.

Exodus 1:15-21 Then Pharoah, the king of Egypt, gave this order to the Hebrew midwives, Shiphrah and Puah: When you help the Hebrew women as they give birth, watch as they deliver. If the baby is a boy, kill him; If it is a girl, let her live. But because the midwives feared God, they refused to obey the king's orders. They allowed the boys to live, too. So the king of Egypt called for the midwives. Why have you done this? he demanded. We have you allowed the boys to live? The Hebrew women are not like the Egyptians women, the midwives replied. They are more vigorous and have their babies so quickly that we cannot get there in time. So God was good to the midwives, and the Israelites continued to multiply, growing more and more powerful. And because the midwives feared God, he gave them families of their own.

We see here it pays to value the relationship you have with the Lord. Being a covenant keeper will get you many benefits.

Spiritual Mentors

Spiritual Mentors are divine connectors and could be considered as one like a Deborah, Samuel to Saul and David, Nathan to David, Elisha to Gehazi, Huldah, Peter to Paul, Barnabas to John Mark and Priscilla and Aquila to Apollos.

Covenant People Versus Divine Connections

Fathers And Mothers In The Gospel Type Of Relationship

Fathers and Mothers is known to be longevity covenant people; such as Abraham and Sarah, Moses to Joshua, Priest Eli to Samuel, Elijah to Elisha, Mary the mother of Jesus was not just known as Jesus mother but Jesus told John the apostle that she is now your mother, Deborah was known as a mother of Zion, Jesus to the disciples, Paul was a father to the churches that he planted and built. Naomi to Ruth.

Deborah And Barak Type Of Relationship

Judge 4:6-9 One day she sent for Barak son of Abinoam, who lived in Kadesh in the land of Abinoam, who lived in Kadesh in the land of Naphtali. She said to him, This is what the Lord, the God, of Israel; commands you: Call out 10,000 warriors from the tribes of Naphtali and Zebulun at Mount Tabor. And I will call out Sisera, commander of Jabin's army, along with his chariots and warriors, to the Kishon River. There I will give you victory over him. Barak told her, I will go, but only if you go with me.

Very well, she replied, I will go with you. But you will receive no honor in this venture, for the Lord's victory over Sisera will be at the hands of a woman. So Deborah went with Barak to Kadesh.

Paul And Priscilla And Aquila Teamwork Type Of Relationship

Acts 18:1-3 Then Paul left Athens and went to Corinth. There he became acquainted with a Jew named Aquila, born in Pontus, who had recently arrived from Italy when Claudius Caesar deported all Jews from Rome. Paul lived and worked with them, for they were tent makers just as he was.

Acts 18:18 Paul stayed in Corinth for some time after that, then said goodbye to the brothers and sisters and went to nearby Cenchrea. There he shaved his head according to Jewish custom, marking the end of a vow. Then he set sail for Syria, taking Priscilla and Aquila with them.

Romans 16:3-5 Give my greetings to Priscilla and Aquila, my co-workers in the ministry of Christ Jesus. In fact, they once risked their lives for me. I am thankful to them, and so are all the Gentiles churches. Also give my greetings to the church that meets in their home.

Elijah And Elisha Type Of Relationship

1 Kings 19:19-20, So Elijah went and found Elisha son of Shaphat plowing in a field. There were twelve teams of oxen in the field and Elisha was plowing with the twelfth team. Elijah went over to him and threw his cloak across his shoulders and then walked away. Elisha left the oxen standing there, ran after Elijah, and said to him, First let me go and kiss my father and mother good-bye, and then I will go with you.

2 Kings 2:1 When the Lord was about to take Elijah up to heaven in a whirlwind, Elijah and Elisha were traveling from Gilgal. And Elijah said to Elisha, Stay here, for the Lord has told me to go to Bethel. But Elisha replied, As surely as the Lord lives and you yourself live, I will never leave you.

2 Kings 2:9-12 When they came to the other side, Elijah said to Elisha, Tell me what I can do for you before I am taken away. And Elisha replied, Please let me inherit a double share of your spirit and become your successor. You have asked a difficult thing, Elijah replied. If you see me when I am taken away from you, then you will get your request. But if not, then you won't. As they were walking along and talking suddenly a chariot of fire appeared, drawn by horses of fire. It drove between the two men separating them, and Elijah was carried by a whirlwind into heaven. Elisha saw it and cried out, My Father, My Father. I see the chariots and charioteers of Israel! And as they disappeared from the sight, Elisha tore his clothes in distress.

David And Jonathan Relationship
1 Samuel 20:12-17, 2 Samuel 9. Could it be possible that David didn't kill King Saul because of the covenant and relationship he

had for Jonathan and not just because of Saul still being the Lord's anointed. David loved Jonathan so much and valued the relationship they had he remember the promises he made to him about showing kindness continually to his children forever. Truly Jonathan and David was honored covenant and were covenant people.

1 Samuel 20:41-42 As soon as the boy was gone, David came out from where he had been hiding near the stone pile. Then David bowed three times to Jonathan with his face to the ground. Both of them were in tears as they embraced each other and said good-bye, especially David. At last Jonathan said to David, Go in peace, for we have sworn loyalty to each other in the Lord's name. The Lord is the witness of a bond between us and our children forever. Then David left, and Jonathan returned to the town.

1 Samuel 9:1 One day David asked, Is anyone in Saul's family still alive-anyone to whom I can show kindness for Jonathan sake?

Covenant People Versus Divine Connections

1 Samuel 9:3-7 The king then asked him, Is anyone still alive from Saul's family? If so, I want to show God's kindness to them. Ziba replied, Yes, one of Jonathan's son is still alive. He is crippled in both feet. Where is he? the king asked. In Lo-debar. Ziba told him, at the home of Makir son Ammiel. So David sent him and brought him from Makirs home. His name was Mephibosheth; he was Jonathan's son and Saul's grandson. When he came to David, he bowed low to the ground in deep respect. David said, Greetings, Mephibosheth. Mephibosheth replied, I am your servant. Don't be afraid! David said. I intend to show kindness to you because of my promise to your father, Jonathan. I will give you all the property that once belonged to your grandfather Saul, and you will eat here with me at the king's table!

Jesus And 11 Disciples Relationship
Luke 6:12-16 One day soon afterward Jesus went up on a mountain to pray, and he prayed to God all night. At daybreak he called together all of his disciples and chose twelve of them to be apostles, Here are their names: Simon

Covenant People Versus Divine Connections

(whom named Peter), Andrew (Peter brother), James, John, Philip, Bartholomew, Matthew, Thomas, James (son of Alphaeus), Simon(who was called the zealot), Judas (son of James), Judas Iscariot (who later betrayed Jesus)

John 17:6-27, "I have revealed to you to the ones you gave me from this world. They were always yours. You gave them to me, and they have kept your word. Now they know that everything I have is a gift from you, for I have passed on to them the message you gave me. They accepted it and know that I came from you, and they believe you sent me. My prayer is not for the world, but for those you have given me, because they belong to you. All who are mine belong to you, and you have given them to me, so they bring me glory. -Now I am departing from the world; they are staying in this world, but I am coming to you. Holy Father, you have given me your name; now protect them by the power of your name so that they will be united just as we are. During my time here, I protected them by the power of the name you gave me. I guarded them so that not

Covenant People Versus Divine Connections

one was lost, except the one headed for destruction, as the scriptures foretold. Now i am coming to you. I told them many things while I was with them in this world so they would be filled with my joy. I have given them your word. And the world hates them because they do not belong to the world, just as I don't belong to the world. I'm not asking that you would take them out of the world, but to keep them safe from the evil one. They do not belong to this world no more than I do. Make them holy by your truth; teach them your word, which is truth. Just as you sent me into the world, I am sending them into the world. And I give myself as a holy sacrifice for them so they can be made holy by your truth. I am praying not only for these disciples but also for all who will ever believe in me through their message. I pray that they will all be one, just as you and I are one-as you are in me, Father, and I am in you. And may they be in us so that the world will believe you sent me. I have given them the glory you gave me, so they may be one as we are one. I am in them and you are in me. May they experience such perfect unity that the world will know that you sent me and that you love them as much as you love me. Father, I want these whom you have given me to be with me where I am. Then they can see all the glory you gave me because you loved me even before the world began! O righteous Father, the world doesn't know you, but I do; and these disciples know you sent me. I have revealed you to them, and I will continue to do so. Then your love for me will be in them, and I will be in them." (NLT)

Jesus And Judas
Judas was divinely connected to Jesus for a divine purpose.

John 13:18-21 I am not saying these things to all of you; I know the ones I have chosen. But this fulfills the Scriptures that says, The one who eats my food has turned against me. I tell you this beforehand, so that when it happens you will believe that I AM the Messiah. I tell you the truth, anyone who welcomes my messenger is welcoming me, and anyone who welcomes me is welcoming the Father who sent me. Now Jesus was deeply troubled, and he exclaimed, I tell you the truth, one of you will betray me!

John 13:30-32 As soon as Judas left the room, Jesus said, The time has come for the Son of Man to enter into his glory, and to be glorified because of him. And since God receives glory because of the Son, he will soon gives glory to the Son.

John 6:70-71 Then Jesus said, I chose the twelve of you, but one is a devil. He was speaking of Judas, son of Simon Iscariot, one of the Twelve, who would later betray him.

Matthew 27:3-8, Then Judas threw the silver coins down in the Temple and went out and hanged himself.

John 17:12, During my time here, I protected them by the power of the name you gave me. I guarded them so that not one was lost, except the one headed for destruction, as the scriptures foretold.

Chapter 6
Prophetic Relationships Versus Political Relationships

Prophetic Relationships

What are Prophetic relationships?
Prophetic Relationships are God inspired that deals with destiny and purpose. These kinds of relationships are those that God joined together. Titus 1:15

Example: Joseph and Mary (Jesus earthly parents). Joseph was a descendant of David. It was already prophesied that Jesus would be a descendant of David. You see it had to do with destiny and purpose. You see this is what prophetic relationships are for it has to do with destiny and purpose. It has to come together for the sake of destiny and purpose. This is the intent of the why God join them together. Matthew 3:13-17...

Prophetic Relationships Versus Political Relationships

You see here John and Jesus had a prophetic destiny. They had to fulfill all righteousness. They had to expose all things that were not right in God sight. So their relationship was God inspired. They just didn't come together, it was intentional by God. It was God plan for them to come together. Luke 1:39-45... Mary and Elizabeth. Prophetic relationships are not hindrances to God purpose on your life. We need to always ask God to send you someone that can make your baby leap. Connect with people that can make destiny leaps within you. Connect with people that can see the potential in you and make it come out that stirs you up when they come around you. I would advise you to ask God to send you some people that will stir you up. You see they are not hindrances to the call on your life. Actually what they do they excite you to it. They turn you on to it. When Mary and Elizabeth got together they were like "YES" I can do this thing now and that's the type of people the enemy is trying to separate you from. You see Prophetic relationships will provoke the enemy. Prophetic relationship is a provoker of political

Prophetic Relationships Versus Political Relationships

relationship. That's why the enemy tries so hard to divide prophetic relationships. He's' tries to separate people that needs to be together. He's' tries to separate you from the place that's exciting you. Satan knows that if you stay within that prophetic relationship in covenant with them your destiny is going to come to pass that includes your destiny stopping him. You see as long as Mary and Elizabeth were hooked up John and Jesus was hooked up. They both had assignments but John went before Him, preparing the way for Jesus. Sometimes we don't know what our destines behold but we have to learn how to recognize, embrace and fight for prophetic relationships that's thrust us further into destiny. They're the key to your growth.

Prophetic people in prophetic relationship have the ability to see beyond the outer exterior even when the outer garments looks raggedy. You see John the Baptist at the reintroduction of Jesus had the ability to see beyond Jesus outer garments and saw the Kings of kings, Lord of lords and the Messiah that is, will be

Prophetic Relationships Versus Political Relationships

and was to come. Something in him leaped as if it was the first day he met and was introduced to Him. Likewise the disciples they looked beyond His outer appearance and heard what bore witness to their spirit man that propelled them to follow Him prophetically. Can somebody say and the baby LEAPED WITHIN THEM!!! Now we see what prophetic relationship is, this the same way for a husband and wife. Before he became her husband she has the ability to see beyond his flaws and weaknesses to be able to pull out the potential within him that will push him to destiny. How can a wife help nurture and build him where he needs to be if he's already perfect and or she doesn't have the ability to see the potential within him. Women we have to have the ability to see what the man hasn't put out there in the opening on display for you and covering up for you to see to pull out. Prophetic people see pass your bling, fame, positions, titles and etc, to be able to get you to destiny. Now lets' venture into political relationships.

Prophetic Relationships Versus Political Relationships

Political Relationships

What is Political Relationship?

Political Relationship is a relationship and covenant that wasn't inspired by God. Most of the times it's inspired by fame, money, statuses, titles, associations, position, power, prestige, name, a sense of peace or for the sake of peace. These relationships are generally formed because of our own desires. So basically they're SOULISH. Political relationship drives you further away from God and the destiny He destined for your life.

These are the relationships that the enemy invoke and promote because its keeping you away from destiny. It's a problem when you have way more political relationships than prophetic relationships. You have way more people that you're connected and linked up to that are not divinely than divinely.

One thing about political relationships they frustrate the grace of God. The grace on your life is for the prophetic relationship. Political relationship evolves in idle talk and babblings

Prophetic Relationships Versus Political Relationships

rather than focusing on your destiny. Political revolves around catering to your soul and broader ways of scheming to get something done for their own selfish reasons. The grace is for the prophetic relationships but you're wasting it on the political relationships. You see the bible tells us that God won't put too much on us than we can bare but a political relationship will put too much on you. You will pick up something that God didn't put on you. Something that God didn't inspire for you to get with and because of picking it up you say God you said you wouldn't put too much on me than I can bare. Well God says I didn't put that on you. I didn't guide you in that place, you went over there, that were your desire and soulish connection that you was trying to connect with and now you have gotten so connected with them it's hard for you to let them go.

The life of King Solomon where we would see many of his political relationships. (1 Kings 4:1-14, 1 Kings 7:13-15, 1 Kings 9:15-28)

Prophetic Relationships Versus Political Relationships

The Presumptuous And Greedy Gehazi's

Prophet Elisha understood that Gehazi wasn't ready for all that the future holds in their relationship. It would've taken more of crucifying self and resisting the pleasures of wealthy and famous. Gehazi zeal was thrusting him to become famous and wealthy in being in relationship with the prophet. He wanted the powers for his own glory and the prophet understood that and warned him many times of his motives and attitude but he didn't take it to heart. Later we see in the story of the relationship of Elisha and Gehazi it came to an end because Gehazi was so greedy to the point of lying on the prophet to get wealthy which ended their relationship and cause him to get leprosy.

2 Kings 5:20-27

But Gehazi, the servant of Elisha, the man of God, said to himself, My master should not have let this Aramean get away without accepting any of his gifts. As surely as the Lord lives, I will chase after him and get something from him. So Gehazi set off after Naaman.

Prophetic Relationships Versus Political Relationships

When Naaman saw Gehazi running after him, he climbed down from his chariot and went to meet him. Is everything all right? Naaman asked. Yes, Gehazi said, but my master has sent me to tell you that two young prophets from the hill country of Ehpraim have just arrived. He would like 75 pounds of silver and two sets of clothing to give to them. By all means, take twice as much silver, Naaman insisted. He gave him two sets of clothing, tied up the money in two bags, and sent two of his servants to carry the gifts for Gehazi. But when they arrived at the citadel, Gehazi took the gifts from the servants and sent the men back. Then he went and hid the gifts inside the house. When he went in to his master, Elisha asked him, where have you been, Gehazi? I haven't been anywhere, he replied. But Elisha asked him, Don't you realize that I was there in spirit when Naaman stepped down from his chariot to meet you? Is this the time to receive money and clothing, olive groves and vineyards, sheep and cattle, and male and female servants? Because you have done this, you and your descendants will suffer from Naaman

Prophetic Relationships Versus Political Relationships

leprosy forever. When Gehazi left the room, he was covered with leprosy, his skin was white as snow.

Greed will destroy relationships! Greed brings curses, not just to you but to your family as well from generation to generation. I've been in a few relationships that were like this and known others in relationships like this. Being in a similar relationship in the past, I've had a friend, a member of our ministry tells me such things that they didn't know I knew by the spirit of the Lord. They continue to lie when I asked them and played innocent as if they didn't do anything. I'm like if you just tell the truth it will be better but they insisted on lying and then swore on the Lord. I watched some of these individuals lives shipwrecked terribly because of greed and lying to and on the Holy Spirit. In watching them I was for-bad strongly by the Lord to not intercede or go try to rescue them, which was hard to do. Your relationship with the Lord God is the most valuable relationship you can have with anyone, so I encourage you to cherish it with every ounce of you.

Prophetic Relationships Versus Political Relationships

Prophetic Relationships that goes wrong because it wasn't nurture because of all the political relationships.

The dangers of political things in prophetic relationships.
1. Settlement- When you just settle for anything and anybody...
2. Peace- Just because it's not a war going on doesn't make it peace. This is where the enemy will try to get you at. You see it going to look like nobody fighting and its peace going on. That don't make it peace but peace is when justice comes. Political relationship says as long as I'm giving you money and you keeping quiet there's peace. If God don't agree with what you're doing then it's not any peace. There's no true peace until justice comes.
3. False Unction's- Something that excites and ignites you to do something good and acceptable.
4. Familiarity- By associations of a big name, because my family in covenant with or I grew up with them. I'm comfortable here and they accept me the way I am.

5. Prestige, Money, People and Fame- When this becomes your focus.

6. Abusing your authority/Mistreatment- When someone in a place of authority will find a time to take advantage of you to promote their agenda. When someone in authority that will belittle, manipulate and dominate you to get you to do something for or submit to them.

Prophetic Relationships that goes wrong because it was nurture wrong.
(1 Kings 5:1-18)

King Hiram had supplied King Solomon with trees, gold and anything Solomon wanted he would make sure Solomon had and it wasn't a problem.On the other hand as soon as he would ask Solomon for something, Solomon would give him something that's good for nothing. Cabul means (unproductive) Good for Nothing...Solomon messed up the relationship. He didn't nurture the relationship right. Have you ever been in a relationship where it been like one-sided. You give all you can give but they're given nothing and not treating you like they want to be treated. Somebody say they

Prophetic Relationships Versus Political Relationships

didn't value the relationship enough. This is not what God intended this relationship to be and go. Solomon short changed him. You will be feeling and asking as Hiram ask Solomon, What have you given me and what kind of cities are these my brother? When you don't value the prophetic relationship you will take it lightly, look over it, nurture it wrong and this will be the result of nurturing the relationship wrong as what happened with Hiram and Solomon. It's a problem when you don't value the relationship then you will began to nurture the wrong relationship right. I've seen it happen too many times where many settled for political relationships putting their all in it to nurture it right and mistreat the prophetic relationship.

1 Kings 9:10-13
It took Solomon twenty years to build the Lord's temple and his own royal place. At the end of that time, he gave twenty towns in the land of Galilee to King Hiram of Tyre. (Hiram had previously provided all the cedar and cypress, timber and gold that Solomon had given him, he was not at all pleased with them. What kind

of towns are these, my brother? he asked. So Hiram called that area Cabul (which means worthless) as it is still known today. Nevertheless, Hiram paid Solomon 9,000 pounds of gold.

Chapter 7
Cultivating Relationships Apostolically

Some of the best relationships you can be in are the ones that you didn't expect to be in. The ones that caught you by surprise. Not the ones that you wished for or wanted to happen but the ones that you didn't expect. Those were the ones that ended up being the best relationships. The ones that came in, tore up your world, tore it down, tore it backwards and front ward, then tore you up too. The end result is those are the ones that end up being the very best relationships. I'm talking about the good ones and the not so good ones. I know you probably saying I know some people that I can do without but guess what "NOT NECESSARILY". We are going to talk about that.

Adam didn't see Eve coming. Abraham didn't see God coming. Moses didn't see God

Cultivating Relationships Apostolically

coming. Barach didn't see Deborah coming. Eli didn't see Samuel coming. Elisha didn't see Elijah. Zechariah didn't see John the Baptist coming. Mary didn't see Holy Spirit & Jesus coming. Joseph didn't see Jesus coming. Elizabeth didn't see Mary coming. The Disciples didn't see Jesus coming. Saul known as Paul didn't see Jesus coming. Some of us can look back over our lives and say we didn't see Jesus coming neither. You know you were doing your own thing and had it going on too. You had your own plans, timeline and agenda saying I'm going to be doing this and that by this time but Jesus showed up.

My testimony of Jesus coming to me surprisingly that I can remember is a day in the fall of October 2002 when I was staying in Millen Georgia. I had a nice shape with plenty of men wanting me but had only one guy friend that I loved that showered me with anything I wanted that I thought was a god. I got my first car which was a black two-door chevy cavalier at the time. I was going to Technical College in Statesboro Georgia. I was also working two jobs at the time, one at a convenience store in Statesboro Georgia, and another one at a Hair Salon in Twin City Georgia. I had plans that when I did turn 21 years old I would be real legal where I can buy alcohol, cigarettes and was able to get in the clubs I wanted but God had different plans for me. I remembered having these dreams about heaven to where I had visions in the dream of Jesus telling me to choose who I will serve, I saw and went to hell in the dream and saw about 12 different types of tornadoes to where I woke up throwing up, dehydrated, barely could see and couldn't walk nor talk. I then pressed my way to get out of bed by falling over out onto the floor, crawling on the floor out the bedroom down the long hallway to reached the living room where my cousin was uttering now like whispers help. When I finally reached her, my voice came back stronger to me a little to be able to tell her what was wrong. She called 911 and her uncle which was a police officer but while we waited on them she took my blood pressure with her machine because was a diabetic. My blood pressure at that time read 240 over 124 both big numbers, somewhere around them numbers or bigger. Now you know I was supposed to be dead. At that time my weight was 160-170 and height was 5'4. Her uncle the police officer came first where he took me to the hospital because he didn't trust the ambulance to get there in time enough. Water couldn't quench my thirst, nor any other liquids. So when I did get to the emergency room they put ivy's of course in me, where there was a doctor that were a Christian came in and began to talk to me about faith. She began to read scriptures to me off index cards that she had, then she gave them to me. To make a long story short this was the new journey of my salvation walk with my Lord. After that I souled out to the Lord. I went to church revivals to where I was getting prophecies. I fled from my boyfriend and family that I stayed with because I knew staying in that house I couldn't stay saved. All of this was shortly after my grandmother died the one that introduced me to Jesus and served the Lord faithfully to her last breath.

Cultivating Relationships Apostolically

We all have a story similar to this to tell how we didn't see the Lord coming. Oh and by the way I didn't have high blood pressure. The doctors ran all kinds of test on me and said I'm in great health. At this time I was regularly exercising. God just saw fit to snatch me out of hell to give me a choice to serve him. I said God you got my attention and I choose Heaven and not hell. The God of Heaven snatched me and you out of the mouth of hell and caught us by surprise and said you are my son and daughter whom I love.

All of that was done, good and fine, but now look at somebody else and say I DARE YOU TOO TO CHANGE!!!

We sing about we want the glory but what you going to do when you get it? Are you going to walk around with it saying, I have the glory. Is your perception of the glory just a feeling, tangling, and quickening? What is it really? Why do you really want it? Is it because that's the trendy kingdom word to say? To have the glory of God is to cultivate relationships apostolically. There's a purpose for the glory, the presence, the power, the eminence of God but when you walk in that am I going to be arrogant and proud saying my life, gift, anointing is more glorified than yours. Ask yourself, what do you want this glory for? Is it for your own consumption? It's like giving a child bag of candy in a whole room full of children and they refuse to share. When you get the glory, are you going to share it? How do you use the glory for the glory of God? Yes, cultivating relationship apostolically.

Let's break some stuff down...

The Purpose of Cultivation

To cultivate means to promote or improve the growth of something by labor and attention. So if I'm going to cultivate something that means I'm going to take some attention and some labor. If I'm going to cultivate a relationship it's going to take some time, attention and labor. If I'm going to give you my attention that my time? Correct? And when I labor that means I'm going to put some labor in to it. Correct?

Cultivating Relationships Apostolically

Our very best effort in a relationship is our relationship with Jesus Christ. The bible says Jesus put in much time and labor for us as sweating drops of blood. So the life of Jesus in essence is cultivating relationships apostolically. He was sent from Heaven to earth to us. Not just to come and scoop us up but He had to work at it. He had to first of all have relationship with us, and then He had to teach us how to have relationship with him. Then He was able to be taken up. The disciples was our/is our example. He came. He called them. He was sent to them. He taught them about Himself and how to have a relationship with the Father. When He taught them this, He took up His cross. Crucified of course, went to the grave, conquered the grave, resurrected and then taken back up to the Heavenly Father which art in Heaven being seated on the right side of Throne. He cultivated the relationship. So when the book of Acts happened all the disciples/apostles do was do what Jesus did. They just did what they were taught., to where the body of Christ was birthed. Now we don't have 12 relationships but we have numerous relationships.

Now Two important words: To Promote and Growth. When we get into a relationship naturally, two things we don't normally do and that is to promote growth. Can we be honest with ourselves? Some people normally would get into a relationship with the mentality of what we can get from them, how you can help me, or how can you help me get further alone. That is exactly the opposite of what it is to cultivate a relationship apostolically. When you cultivate, you improve the growth of relationship of someone else in Christ and you develop them so that they can flourish, advance and go to the next level and position. When I cultivate something I refine it. They mean to bring it to a fine or pure state. That is why I said initially that some of the best relationship is those that are least to be expected. The good ones and not so good ones, because those tore up people that God allows to come into your life are the ones that even sent to refine you. To pull out and to draw out the impurities. Have you ever notice those seemly devilish people that are sent into your life and you rebuke, bind them and cast the devil out of them but the devil don't move but he stay right up in your face, given you problems after problems. Everywhere you turn the devil given you problems at your job, problems at your house, and everywhere you look you're having problems but the only time that devil moves is when you turn introspect to yourself and say God what do I do to change. Am I right about it?

When you turn the situation around and you say ok now God I'm going to look at them even though their causing me trouble but what it is about me and my heart that has to change because obviously there's something that I'm not getting here? You see, when you realize that relationship was sent apostolically to you to help refine you. You see, when you realize that as much as God loves me, as He did Job, He still allowed that devil to be used for my good. But, it wasn't until I said as long as I live I'm going to wait until my change comes. I will not accuse the Lord of wrong doings but I will look unto the Lord from which my help comes from. My help that comes from the Lord, meaning help has come to change me. Those people in your life that has come to provoke you, has come to refine you, change you, cultivate you and get you to the next place of holiness. Causing you to walk in righteousness, getting on your face seeking God like you never sought the Lord before. He knows that all is going well you're not going to give him time because of your comfortability and relaxation.

The Lord moves sideways because you don't really understand the reason why you're in this position or why you're where you are. So He says I will just shake up some things so you can seek me, so that you want stay in kindergarten for the next 3 years, because you like to camp out and you don't camp out in 10th grade. You don't camp out in college and so when its' time to graduate, if you don't have the curriculum that's right here in this place. Curriculum you know the stuff you suppose the study, the homework you suppose to do, and those test you suppose to pass. Since God is not into a C GPA or remedial treatment when it comes to class and His bride, He will continue to refine you until you get pearly gold. God is cultivating you to be special and not slow in knowledge and understanding of Him.

There are times in our lives in these seemly chaotic relationships, we will say God, I'm done Lord, I'm not helping them no more and they have gotten on my last nerve. That's when He reminds us of Galatians 5:22 which are the fruit of the spirit. You will have to draw on that patience, on that long-suffering, draw on that self-control along with tolerance and endurance. When I say you will draw on it. You will begin to call it up on the inside of you. Not in a continuance of speaking in tongues but saying Father right now in the name of Jesus, I possess the fruit of the spirit. So I call on the fruit of the spirit now and I call on patience to be at work within me in my heart and soul right now in the name of Jesus. Then you go about your way and have patience within you to have it perfect work. Father I thank you for endurance. You have given me endurance because you have given me your spirit. I call on it to manifest in this relationship right now because I am here in this relationship because they are going to grow and I'm going to grow too. Cultivating relationships apostolically.

When I speak of refining, I speak of you freeing yourself and the other person from impurities. You purifies from what is coarse or hard, vulgar, debasing or degrading. Ask yourself is there anything in your life that needs to be purified? When it means to be refined or have ourselves to be refined, it means to be or make ourselves PRECISE and ACCURATE. In this place of being refined, precise and accurate, is when someone may come and mislabel you, you won't be moved or shaken but you will not become the unshakable kingdom that will stand. No one won't determine or dictate who you are but you and your relationship with Jesus Christ that you have cultivated now will determine it and make you precise.

So when those demons and devils that God has allowed to come into my life, I won't be moved because I know they have a purpose. That purpose is not to do me in or do me out but to help me up. They were sent to help me up. What about the people that came into your life that started out good in your life but then they end up bad? What about the relationship that started out well but ended up sour? Could it be that God touched the heart of the king? The bible says the heart of the king is in the hands of the Lord. Could it be that that's the king's heart He touched that turned against you just so that now you thought you was standing up straight all by yourself but actually you was leaning on them. So He has to move your own little crutch. Every time you needed assistance you called sister Goodfoot because she's a praying woman of God and she's a prophet of God. You know she hears the word of the Lord for you and you say she's my prophetess. I can call her for a word anytime but now the Lord moves sister Goodfoot. It just so happens she started a rumor about you in the church. You don't understand why sister goodfoot said this about you because you never done anything to harm her but now all of a sudden she's against you. She influenced some others to be against you as well. Now you need a word from the Lord. You was walking with two feet leaning on sister goodfoot but now she's been moved from being your crutch. You then find yourself hopping on one foot, not being able to find your balance. Until you discovered that you have another. It been there all along but you didn't know you had another foot because you was leaning on sister goodfoot. When she was moved, you finds out you have two feet. You begins to adjust yourself position and finds some strength in the side that you was leaning on sister goodfoot. So now because you can longer call her to get a word, you decide you will stand up to the God of your salvation. Seek His Face. Turn from your wicked ways. Then He heals your lands and gives you a word of strength and encouragement. You now finds out that you don't have to be mad with sister goodfoot, because when she was move out of the way you found out her moving out was to help move you up. Moving them out is to move you up. So now it's time to repent of your bitterness. Release your unforgiveness, for all the people that have turned against you and you didn't do any harm to them. You don't know why your name has been made mud. You don't know why you had to leave the church. You don't know why the family doesn't like you no more. You don't know why the people on the job have turned against you. I come to tell you that when you forgive and release even now, you will not just be moved out but He'll move you up.

When you realize their purpose and let them go the quicksand will release you. God was only trying to refine you. You don't know why that preacher turned against you. You don't know why certain people turned against you or started the rumor but now I know its' supposed to be for my good. So now I say to you to take this time, stop and think on those people that you need to release. As I said before I say now, I DARE YOU TO FORGIVE AND RELEASE THEM. FORGIVE AND RELEASE THEM.

Father I thank you as your people are forgiving right now. I thank you Lord that you are uprooting roots of bitterness. I thank you that you're snatching roots of bitterness out of their souls and you are exchanging roots of bitterness with love, redemption and forgiveness. Sadness, mourning and sorrow for oil of gladness and joy. The spirit of heaviness for the garment of praise. A broken spirit and broken heart for a cheerful heart and renewed spirit.

Part 2 of Cultivating Relationships Apostolically

Leadership Preparing You for Service (Ephesians 4:11-13)

There comes a time where you will be tested and learn how to respect leadership and treat them properly. Not just with your lips service and with your actions, but having proper honor in your heart and with your attitude. If you don't properly align the honor in your heart and attitude, you will be served in a way that you don't want to be served. Meaning you will cause yourself hardships, because they were sent to prepare you and the body. Now you can fight being prepared all you want because as long as you fight against being prepared you going to stay stuck. As long as you fight against God sent to prepare you, you will be idle. The very things God has delivered you from, you're open yourself back up too, because you're opposing leadership. You see, they were sent apostolically to prepare you for the work of service. Now they can tell you to do one thing but you decide to go do something else. You're not being prepared because you are not following instructions.

It was He that gave them to you. SN: Now if you're not in the right church, please move, because you know what God have told you. Cultivating Relationships Apostolically meaning leaders not going to fool with your foolishness. This is why you need apostles coupled with prophets and pastors. While the pastors busy patting you on the back, you need apostles and prophets giving you tough love that's going to tell you to get up off your bottom and do what you know to do is right. You are not 2 years old. So pull in your bottom lip. It was HE that sent you to the church they was already there. So it was you who was sent apostolically to the church, who the Father sent the leader to that church for you. So that means because you was sent there, you need to get that rebellion worked up out of you.

Ephesian 4:12 says to prepare God people for the work of service. When you resist your preparation, you're saying I'm really not God's people. You must be prepared so that the body of Christ must be equipped and perfected. It is to build the whole body up. If you're not prepared then we are not build up. What is hindering us for getting built up? Could it be you fighting against your preparation?

Don't be so anxious and fast to leave proper care and training that you miss a step in your preparation and lack growth. Are possibly you're not at the step you think you're arrived at. You're not as grown as you think you are. You know how the old folks used to tell us, you not as grown as you think you are. Yes, you may look grown or maybe the age 21 but still not grown. We must all mature in the unity of faith so we can attain the measure of Christ.

Now you know how vital it is to cultivate relationship apostolically.

Chapter 8
Sonship

Before you can be positioned into any office, you must first become a son going through the proper training of sonship. Sonship is the highest level of discipleship.

True Sons are in a real relationship with their Father.

Sons recognize that before they can become a father they first have to become a son.

Sonship is a process that goes through the stages of a baby, a boy, a man, a disciple then son. Before Jesus Himself the Son of Man had to go through these proper stages on earth as well that show us the examples of the and process of sonship. Jesus started off as being a baby, then a boy where his earthly parents was looking for him, then man, then discipleship being tempted by satan then the

Father spoke and said this my son in whom I am well please with.

The Stages of Sonship from a baby to a son.

1st stage the BABY-Luke (NLT) 2:16,21 says They hurried to the village and found Mary and Joseph. And there was the BABY, lying in the manger.

Luke 2:21 (NLT) Eight days later, when the BABY was circumcised, he was named Jesus, the name given him by the angel even before he was conceived.

2nd stage the BOY- Luke 2:43 (AMP) And when the Feast was ended, as they were returning, the BOY Jesus remained behind in Jerusalem. Now His parents did not know this.

3rd stage the MAN

4th stage the DISCIPLE

5th stage the SON- Luke 3:21 (NLT) One day when the crowds were being baptized. As he was praying, the heavens opened, and the Holy Spirit, in bodily form, descended on him like a dove. And a voice from heaven said, You are my dearly loved SON, and you bring me great joy.

How can you become a father without being fathered? How can you want others to be submitted and obedient to you when you haven't been submitted, committed or obedient yourself?

If you don't have a relationship with God you want be able to have a relationship with your father in the gospel.

LET ME HELP YOU BECOME A SON AND PRODUCE MUCH MORE FRUIT OF BEING A SON

Becoming A Son
Sons uphold the standard of true doctrine and teach others the standards.
Sons begats and make sons.
Sons have a love from a pure heart.
Sons are not hypocritical.
Sons avoid idle talk.

Sonship

Son's motivation is from a pure heart of love and they don't seek their own agenda.
Sons are teachers of the law and sound doctrine.
Sons obtain greater mercy and grace because of their love and obedience.
Sons are faithful, full of faith and love.
Sons fight a good fight of faith.
Sons exposes wicked and evil people and their wickedness in the mist then put them out of the fellowship of the saints.
Sons earnestly become seekers of prayer.
Sons exercise control and practice righteousness.
Sons endure hardship because of his faith.
Sons bring edification to the believers.
1 John 3:12, Rev 21:7, 2 Sam 7:14, Matt 5:9, 8:12, 2 Cor 6:17-18, Luke 16:8, 6:35, 1 Thess 5:5, 1 Tim 1:3, Gal 3:26
Sons are sent ones-apostolic.

Sons understand submission.
Many try to avoid the word submission because of the abuse of it. Submission is a touchy subject in the body of Christ because of

Sonship

the abuse of authority. However, submission is not submission if we agree, but submission is when I say something to you when you don't agree or have the total understanding of it but yet in still yield your will too it.

Sonship is not kissing up. True sons are not intimidated by other sons and daughters, because they understand that there is enough to go around. True sons looks for a long-term relationship and not short term. True sons know how to honor and value their overseers. True sons is about serving with no reward or applaud attach to it. True sons will make sure the overseers taking care of and make sure their parents in the gospel have no need of anything. As you honor the anointing on the life of the overseer you will get more. This is how you draw impartation from them. True sons have the right attitude of the heart when they give unto and serve their leaders. True sons will have a desire to sow generously into the lives of their leader's lives materialistic as the woman that gave all she had to Christ Jesus which was fifteen cents.

Sonship

Ask yourself; Are you familiar with your father vision and the work of the ministry? Do you promote the ministry?

Sons are familiar with their father's vision and make sure they carry the vision out and make sure their known in the gates. True sons promote the vision of the house and won't let anything outside of the vision of the house come into the house. True sons make sure they don't have an agenda to promote their own agenda but on the contrary have their own vision to die so the vision of the house and fathers could live. True sons will defend the house and protect it at all cost. If you are a true son you don't criticize them or comment every time they make decisions, changes, and suggestions. True sons don't re-evaluate everything their father in the gospel say to see if it's God or not, because a true son understand the level of submission that he must do to carry out his father will. A true son understands that God nor his father in the gospel is not up for re-election, nor do they need his approval, vote or opinion but because

Sonship

of a True father he considers his son and don't take advantage of him. A son understands his purpose is to carry out the will of the father. Abraham reproduced himself through Isaac. Isaac reproduced himself through Israel. Moses reproduced himself through Joshua. Naomi reproduced herself through Ruth. Elijah reproduced himself through Elijah. The Heavenly Father reproduced Himself through Jesus. Jesus the Christ reproduced himself through the Disciples. Apostle Paul reproduced himself through Timothy and Titus and the list goes on.

Can you write down the vision of the house in your local church at least one word? If so, is it apart of your spirit?

I've heard many say that they were a part of a well-known mega preacher, to where they sowed big money into them, protected them to the core, made them known in the gates and was enthuse about them but was a member of so and so church, where their pastor prays for and labor for them tremendously. How is it that

Sonship

you can do all of this for the mega church preacher but you a member to so and so church? It's time to check and examine your sonship.

A father hates to build on another man foundation; better yet he will not do it. The father will tear down and uproot that old way to build what he requires of you to carry out for him to do because he will not be able to fully trust you with your or someone else's agenda and vision, knowing that its coinciding in your vision. He will then have to go through the rebuilding process of being a son.

Some people have heap up themselves many instructors that have caused them to be unstable. A son understands the importance of instructors, mentors and multitudes of counselors but realizes the severity, value and benefits of the Father in his life. I've seen people struggled with growing and maturing in the things of Lord being under their covering while others that wasn't a part of their fold but submitted and respected the covering of that father grow rapidly, and this is because only a son can receive the true portion and increase. There are people that come in with their own agenda having the honeymoon phrase (6 months period). They will began showing how gifted they are. They will submit and obey to everything you say until that day that you tell them no, it's not the time or you can't preach today and boi will they show you who they really are.

You don't have to go chasing after a true son on Sunday or any other church events because sons understand commitment. In fact, a son will be the first or about the first one in the church that will even call you to ask about the events if something comes up or tells you of their absence. You won't have to continue to remind a son about his duties and responsibilities because they want what on their leader's life and they want it because they want to go to another level.

Sons are familiar with the work of their father in the gospel. Sons understand that they should be imitating their father but not cloning him. A true son would obey when his father tell him not to do something without bucking against it, because he knows that his father has his best interest at heart. True sons don't have their own vision, agenda or ministry and they won't let outsiders bring in a vision contrary to the vision of their father. True sons will defend their father and his house.

Schisms in the body say I understand what she/he saying but this is how I see and feel about it. Schisms criticize everything their father or mother in the gospel does or say and always has a two way of seeing it. Schisms have to comment on everything every time their leaders say something, by re-evaluating everything they say or decide to step out to do.

Sons have similarities of their father, although personalities are different. True sons understand the importance of honor. What is honor? It is describing value. Sons don't give honor to get accolades, credit or be put on a pedestal. True sons understand that you should give and serve without letting others know about it. So if you're looking for a pat on the back every time you do something then you need to question and examine your motives and sonship. True sons rather have the mantle and anointing on their lives than a thank you. Sonship is about a spiritual relationship. True sons will make sure their leaders never lacking in their natural lives. True Sons want to sow and give always to their leaders and its' not about the amount you give but the honor that's shown. As you honor the father you draw on the anointing that's in them.

Characteristics Of Sonship
1). True sons can identify their fathers and mothers in the gospel.
2). True sons are submitted to their father.
3). True Sons obey the instructions of their father.
4). True sons honor their father.
5). True sons adore and embrace the chastening of their father.
6). True sons are faithful and loyal to their father.

7). True sons cover the nakedness of their father.

Nakedness of the fathers is when you walking in relationship with your father that when you see the weaknesses of your father, you know or should not speak about it, ridicule him, assault him but take his weaknesses before the throne of God interceding on his behalf. In some cases when his weaknesses is shown to you, you should act as if you never saw it and take it before the Lord in prayer and in different cases it would be wise to come to your father and advise him on the matter. You may ask,,why would I want to cover my father? Well the answer to that is because there will be a day when you yourself will need your nakedness covered. The principle of reaping and sowing remains; you will reap what you sow.

Benefits Of A Son
1). True sons will grow faster spiritually, than if they were on their own. A committed loyal son will grow faster.

Sonship

2). True sons is nurtured and developed under the loving arms of their father in the gospel. Therefore the growth rate will increase faster.
3). True sons will avoid the pitfalls of a previous generation because of his willingness to submit to the counsel of his father,
4). True sons will have a place of protection and covering in storms of life in the ministry. True Fathers will also cover their sons in their time of adversity.
5). True sons can mark and launch their ministry from the momentum of their spiritual father. True fathers will help their sons get their ministry off the ground, by providing an opportunity for them to minister.

ISHMAEL- The bond-son... Hagar had the wedlock son but Sarah had the promise son. Are you trying to go out and lay with someone else to produce a son? True sons shun disloyalty and understand the vitality and importance of being loyal. I pray that in this chapter you have grasped a greater perception of what sonship is and how valuable it is.

Chapter 9
Testings of the Relationships

There will come a time to where every relationship will have to go through the refiner's fire to see if it can endure and stand the test of time. I call it the survival mode. Many have failed the testing because they didn't recognize and understand the purpose of the storm that was sent by God to see if the relationship can stand the pressures of the test. Things may happen where one person may act unseemly during the testing because of the pressure. One person may recognize the purpose of it and one may not but when that happens it takes the more mature person to not fold under pressure but to apply wisdom then take a new approach to the rebuttal person.

I've been in many relationships with women where many have folded and even given up under pressure.

Testings of the Relationships

There was a time where God gave me and my sister in Christ a dream about the storm that was coming to beat upon our relationship and how this storm was setting us up for promotion but when it came she didn't recognize it because of the way it came, even when I reminded her of the storm, but instead she misunderstood it and me, then turned and attacked me the one that was there when no one else was. My approach in this matter after given her words of wisdom and words of encouragement, was that to give her some time to come to herself by given her space. This was the wisdom I've gain and the value that I saw in the relationship as a way to preserve the relationship before it take a reckless impact.

Remembering the time when God would give me words of correction and hard sayings to my friend, but as much I tried to instruct in love with words seasoned with grace she still would perceive it as I was attacking her. I looked at this situation at the time and said how can she misunderstood and misinterpret something was address so plain and clear, but I had to look beyond the surface and perceived that there was an enemy behind the scene that was causing her to remain in bondage where her character was so flawed. I did recognize that God was dismantling her fears and insecurities that it was causing her to be so unstable in her emotions to where she really needed help, deliverance and inner healing. In my time trying to restore my sister was extremely challenging but because I knew my purpose and the value of being in the relationship, I endured the pressures of it.

There was a time when people would speak negative of her to get me to give up on her and even speak negative of me to her but because we knew what they was trying to do, it didn't move us and cause us to show ill feelings towards one another. Being the person that I am which is a fighter, I don't give up on people easily because I know the value of the people that God sends into my life. I cherish moments dearly to my heart.

Testings of the Relationships

Will you be able to endure the suffering of the relationship, such as corrective criticism, outbursts, persecution from others, no money, accusations and etc, or will you stand there and let the enemy tear apart what you all have put much effort and labor in knowingly God said its' all for purpose? We have to begin as well to see when God has sent the storm to cause our relationship to be stronger or when the enemy has plotted a trap to sow discord in our hearts against one another to attack one another to cause us to separate from one another beforetime, by aborting the cause, purpose & promises of the relationship.

There are times when you are called to a hurting and wounded individual, and when this is the case you don't want to act rashly by wanting to give up on the person because of the outbursts and assaults of the person. In this case you will have to show so much patience and see beyond their outburst as a cry for help, taking the necessary steps in restoring them to help in love. Yes, it's not going to be easy, in fact a challenge but you

Testings of the Relationships

can endure this, because believe it or not, what happening in them is producing much more fruit in you to set you up for promotion. So in them even wanting to give up every week and coming back may seem like a draining and waste-less time but this is for your good and if God has told you to not give up and says that its a process of their healing then endure this trial and test because it's producing and birthing something greater beyond this capacity of your life. Endure this, stand still and strong in the mist of this storm, because for surely it will be all worthy in the end. Now ask yourself is this worth fighting for? Ask yourself is this person and relationship worthy enough to save?

Endure and pass the test. Remember God won't put more on you than you can bear. You will know when God wants you to draw back and stop, if it becomes too difficult. In the meantime don't give up when God hasn't release you because the grace is sufficient for you and the test is a set up for promotion. Amen.

Chapter 10
<u>**Strengths and Weaknesses**</u>

In any relationship, you will see its and the person strengths and weaknesses. In seeing weaknesses, never omit or overlook character flaws of another. When going into building a relationship with someone, I will ask God what are the person's weaknesses and strengths to better help them and draw from them. I would advise everyone to do the same. This will too guard your heart from future attacks and will teach you how to better help restore the individual to health and even be restored by the individual. Now when asking the Lord to reveal the weaknesses of the individual and He does it's not for you to take their weaknesses and flaws and use it against them, belittling them or even ignoring them. Their weaknesses is shown to you so that you would take them before the Lord in prayer and seeking the Lord wisdom and instruction to help your brother and sister to be restored back to health in love

Strengths and Weaknesses

through words of correction. It's also shown to you for the protecting of your heart, how far to go with them, how to speak words of comfort, how to wise in your actions setting a righteous example with a holy lifestyle before them so that you cause them to stumble and fall.

My mistakes in ministering to hurting women and men alike is when seeing their weaknesses I threw away their weaknesses and focused only on their strengths, then gave them too much liberty where it then turned around and bit me. Also I began to become too comfortable being too transparent telling too much of my weaknesses with them where it also came around and tore me in pieces. If you do this it will eventually turn around for the worst, so please learn from my mistakes.

As I said before, in seeing their weaknesses it's not for you to take their flaws that has been revealed to you by God or them and use it against them to neither belittle, abuse nor spitefully use them, because this is not love and shows that you truly don't value the

Strengths and Weaknesses

relationship. If you truly value the relationship you will cover and complement them through your strengths in their weaknesses.

When seeing how strong the strengths are in a person that you're in a relationship with, it's not for you to neither do away with their weaknesses nor use their gifts for your personal gain. Their strengths are there to strengthen and compliment you in your weaknesses and also to enrich, increase, sharpen and improve you to produce more fruit.

Chapter 11
<u>Humility Exposes Pride</u>

In your area of leading others you will begin to see the student act in disobedience and rebuttal against you and one of the reason is because partially of your servitude to your previous leaders and mentors was rebuttal and disobedience. Its take humility to see this. You must always remain humble seeing your imperfections in your student to be able to show mercy and grace to them to even minister out of a place of effectiveness and healing, so that deliverance and inner healing can come to the both of you.

When you begin to reach your high peak you will began to see from a different perspective, which I call the aerial view. In the aerial view, others may want you to become the old you and do it the same way but because of your position of authority and assignment it won't let you become the old man by coming down, instead it will cause you to put a demand on the relationship to come higher.

There's a transition because of the shift in the position. When you become a King or Queen, some can get close to you and others have to go through the proper protocol to reach you because of the power in position. There's a level of responsibility that comes with the office in position immediately. This position places you to begin to see things from an aerial view and not with the same view as before.

Your response will either bring dishonor or honor to the one you represents and the one that has trained you.

What's choking your planted seed?

Pride is one of the ways the chokes out the seed that been planted. I've seen many humble people that took a different approach in humility to where it exposed many prideful people that seemly looked humble. There are times where pride is so concealed that you will

Humility Exposes Pride

never know it's there until a time of true humility and the spirit of truth present. Many have operated in false humility for so long that it became a part of their personality and they were ignorant to it, until the appointed time of exposure to where true humility came to uncover pride. I, myself, have operated in false humility to where I found out that it was pride hidden openly.

I've seen where God exposed so many prideful people in relationships that said they were humble. In the humble position in a relationship you will always see the sneaky yet obvious enemy known as pride. In seeing this enemy in a relationship you will have to ask God how to go about it in your approach knowingly pride going to stumble. So God give you the wisdom how to handle a matter in taking a different approach that is humility so you too want fall into the same category as well pride. In your approach of humility you will truly see pride exposed.

Humility Exposes Pride

Its vital not to let pride robbed the relationship of it's value. Although you have something to offer the other also has something to offer. Although you saw some flaws in them, they saw some flaws in you but gave you grace. Remember never think of yourself higher than you ought too because pride and haughtiness has a great fall.

Chapter 12
Self-Worth

Valuing Yourself

When you don't value yourself you will allow others to devalue and steal from you, then you will brush it off as if you didn't see nothing and then esteem them higher than yourself by a continuance of sowing more into them, letting them take advantage of you. I remember when this woman of God came to my house recommended by my husband on a Saturday night because she wanted help and deliverance. I did do personal deliverance on her, prophesied to her, consoled her and gave her counsel about getting wisdom in her giving. That night she asked to come under my mentorship where I told her to seek God about this earnestly before committing to my mentorship because I didn't want her to make a rash and hasty decision because how hurt she was from her former pastor. I gave her specific instructions and details of what my

Self-Worth

mentorship entails. She did ask to come to church with us that Sunday where we visited this church that our local church was in fellowship with. That Sunday at church the pastor called her out, prophesied to her and told her that she need wisdom in her giving because people tends to take advantage of her giving to where she will give everything away. She needed wisdom in her giving. Later on I began to teach her about gaining wisdom in giving and sowing on the right ground, timing and seasons to sow so that her seed want get choked out.

In ministering to this woman of God I saw myself of course because this is what happened to me several times but I focused more on helping her overcome this stage.

You see in every level of your life you will have to master a stage of sowing and giving because there will always be people that comes to glean from you that don't give honor to you, steal from you depreciating your gift.

Self-Worth

I've seen so many like myself let others take advantage of them, because of not seeing the worth in our own self as we think we are seeing. People that I invested in, that depreciated my gift and I began to reap the same penalty as they done to me by the people that they link up with and people that they mentored but still they didn't humble themselves enough by coming to grips to see it. I've seen people lose everything from clothes to houses, cars, people, friends, flock, churches, jobs, companies, children and etc, but still didn't come to apologize to me, the other leaders nor came to self. These people were the people that spoke out of their mouths that they respect and value me and our relationship. I saw Leaders demand things from their members when them themselves wasn't sowing or valuing the relationships that we were in.

We must be very careful of this hypocrisy because it will come back at a time when you will least expect it to, where you should see yourself in the matter as the sword proceeds out of your mouth. I can recall a time at a summit where this apostle asked me something and out of my mouth came devalue and no self-worth. She then told me to see her after service to where she sat me down and chastised me then told me that God wants me to know and see the value in myself, because I have so much to offer. She said also told me that before I can go forth into overseeing and establishing this mass company of women, I had to see my own self-worth. She was very transparent with me and said she saw herself in me and knew I didn't meant to say what I said but God was revealing something to redeem me. She gave me examples of herself, illustrations and instruction about self-worth and to not let people take advantage of me any longer. She changed my life for the greater good and from that day forth I was never the same woman.

Don't let people dictate who you are or what you have invested in you because of how great they think they are. Know your worth, because you too have something to offer. Don't become

Self-Worth

a slave to them. I had to see the value in myself to be able to put a demand on the relationships and person that said they truly respect, love, and valued me. There's a time that will truly come when it will be tested to see if they value you as they say they do. I've chased numerous of people because I didn't see the value in myself even though I knew who I were and what I had to offer but I didn't put a demand on people to sow and invest back into me. I was so caught up in freely giving being drain and all but watching what I give to them they turn and give to others what I shared with them and then give the others credit and respect for what I gave them. Now I'm not coming out of a bitter place but giving you wisdom how to be wise in your giving whether it is money, time, food or etc. Be wise in your giving. Yes the word tells us to freely give, freely receive and all of that good stuff but don't let others take advantage of you. You have the right to put a demand on the relationships you're in. It's your right to do so. It's your right to put a demand on the relationship by speaking and having them to sow into you.

If you don't respect yourself, neither will anyone else. Your actions and your time are very valuable. You can be a talking proverb all day long but you must begin to apply that same wisdom to self and see the value in your own self. Yes, there's a time in our life when we must freely give and freely receive but there's a time where you will have to put a demand on the flock/people how Apostle Paul and Apostle Peter done. During your time of putting a demand on the relationship, you will become misunderstood and criticize as a money hungry person but be encourage because it your right to do so.

I've seen so many leaders lose much, cry and be drain by people that didn't value them as they said they did. Some may know them as false brethren, pimps, abusers of authority, and stiff-necked, unbelievers, but be encourage and know you value just as much.

Chapter 13
Choosing Among Commitments

It is very wise to choose among commitments. Many has jumped in quickly and agreed to too many commitments in relationships without thinking what the consequences will be and all that it may require. I've seen many people get into many relationship and making commitments rashly forgetting that they has already committed to something else. I've seen some commit to something where they knew they needed rest. I've seen some where they quickly agreed to something not realizing that there are others that are involved. I've seen many rush into commitments where they neglected their families, love ones and other major responsibilities. This is why its very vital to be slow to speak and quick to listen, so that you will carefully analyze the whole situation to see if it's wise to take upon yourself this commitment, so that you won't have to regret it later.

Choosing Among Commitments

All commitments are not bad at all, it just when you know that when committing to something, it will require focus, time and dedication. Also in your choosing among the commitment, you should examine the motive, in which it will bring glory too or if it goes against everything you believe and stand for.

In Exodus 1:8-21, the midwives had a choice to obey the law of the Pharaoh or disobey him; they chose to disobey him but still were in obedience to God. So they were in a decision making situation to choose a commitment, whether, to obey man law or God law. They chose God. They obeyed the higher power of God Almighty who reigns on the throne. They feared the Lord only. They were committed to the Lord and serve him only even though the Governor spoke something threatens but they made the right choice. The Pharaoh was upset with the midwives because they disobeyed him breaking man law but followed and feared God law.

Choosing Among Commitments

<u>Preparing For Commitment</u>
In Judges 13:1 the Israelites was always disobeying the Lord by worshipping other gods and idols even when the Lord had chosen leaders and judges for them to lead them out of war they would still disobeyed the leaders and God. So the Lord had to once more punish them. You would think they would have had enough chastening by now. But this time the Lord had to put Philistines over the Israelites for 40 years to reign, because of their disobedience.

For Lo and behold, there came another time where God wanted to render deliverance to His people after the oppression of the law of the land so He saw fit to birth and raise up a deliverer to deliver His people from the hands and bondage of the taskmaster. So then there came a time where He opened up another barren womb Samson mother.

Judges 13:1-3 NLT, Again the Israelites did evil in the Lord's sight, so the Lord handed them over to the Philistines, who oppressed them for forty years. In those days a man

Choosing Among Commitments

named Manoah from the tribe of Dan lived in the town of Zorah. His wife was unable to become pregnant, and they had no children. The angel of the Lord appeared to Manoah's wife and said, Even though you have been unable to have children, you will soon become pregnant and give birth to a son.

Manoah wife was barren for some time, but the Lord had to raise up a leader for his people again. Manoah wife received a visitation from the Lord angel that she would bare a son. So she had to get prepared for this commitment from the Lord. This reminds me of myself of what I will have to do to get prepared for my son/child as God has promised. My womb has been shut up and barren for some time but I've been promised by the Lord that I would give birth through my natural womb to a natural son and daughter. I'm still holding on to my promises knowing that they will be deliverers like their parents. I've prepared some and still in preparation for the awaiting time of conception, holding on to the promises of the Lord.

Choosing Among Commitments

You see when a woman is barren it is all for a purpose from the Lord that the womb was shut up for a time to breakthrough to bring forth a deliverer into the earth. Its biblical history of how the barren wombs will breakthrough and break forth in the song of deliverance, that the child will be known as a great leader over nations and also a Deliverer that will bring out nations. So just know that barrenness is for purpose. It may look bad but encourage yourself as I do in the Lord that we the now barren wombs will see the promises fulfilled and bring forth a great deliverer.

Spiritually any seed that you have been promised by the Lord and now are carrying, just know that it will be great. So prepare yourself for spiritual growth, increase and promotion, even in leadership.

Spiritual Barrenness- Spiritual Barrenness can be seen as a Wilderness, Unproductive and Secluded place. There are times where some go through this and don't understand that it was a setup by God to bring and spring forth greatness. In this place, some times of uncertainty, despair, discouragement and hopelessness it's wise to get around people that has been in a barren place but broke through it. It's also good to get around people that are barren as yourself but with hope and great faith that are carrying a great seed to where to they can help encourage and strengthen you.

The angel of the Lord starts to give her (Samson mother) an assignment how to nourish herself in this pregnancy. He told her that she was to keep her body holy unto the Lord and what not to give him nor defile herself with.

Judges 13:4 & 5 NLT... So be careful; you must not drink wine or any other alcoholic drink nor eat any forbidden food. You will become pregnant and give birth to a son, and his hair must never be cut. For he will be dedicated to God as a Nazarite from birth He will begin to rescue Israel from the Philistines.

Choosing Among Commitments

Spiritually when you're pregnant with promotion for leadership, you should be getting prepared by nourishing that seed with prayer, fasting and studying the word of God, writing out the vision. Don't abort your seed or have a miscarriage because of not nourishing your seed and following the necessary instructions that was given and by all means don't you get mad with God because of delayed promises because of your lack of preparation. The angel gave her instructions of what to do before pregnancy, during pregnancy and after the son was to be born on how to raise him up to deliver the people out of bondage. In this spiritually, God is also showing us how to maintain deliverance.

Later on, Manoah wife came to him to share with him about what the Lord angel had said by coming to her with the promise seed. There are times in the bible, where God comes to women first, to bring or deliver a message, not just all the times men. For example: Sarah was alerted and saw the Ishmael mocking Isaac and knew the inheritance of Isaac was threatened. Hagar was met by the angel of the Lord that blessed Ishmael and gave him his name. Hannah was spoken to by the Lord through the blessing of Priest Eli about the birth of Samuel Deborah was spoken to by the Lord about the victory of Israel and call forth the commander Barak to go into battle. Mary Magdalene was the first to see Jesus after his resurrection to give a message to apostles. Mary, the mother of Jesus, was visited by the angel of the Lord the birth of the Messiah.Tabitha, the prophetess, foresaw and prophesied Jesus birth. There are times God would let the wife be the first to know but he would confirm it with the husband which is the head too. So husbands and leaders don't be intimidated when God shows it to the women first. This doesn't mean that she's higher than you but it just the fact that God want to break tradition, she was available at the time and God has no respecter of persons for He chooses as He wills.

Manoah wanted confirmation from the Lord also which was a wise thing to seek the Lord

Choosing Among Commitments

first about. It was wise to seek the Lord about this promise and to make the better decisions as being the Head, and for the nourishment of the seed that she was to carry as well as herself. In my opinion Manoah may was a little jealous of his wife in this situation. I also think Manoah was a busy working man. God always checked a person motives and faith level and in this case I believed He did Manoah. We do see where Manoah wanted more of the instructions on how to take care of his wife and the child, so both could be taken care of properly as the Lord had commanded. So she could beware of how to nourish herself and the child.

In many instances you will see the husband be instructed the more how to protect, provide, love and care for his wife especially in the time of conception. He has to be very considerate of her needs, by being sensitive and patient of her hormonal shift and changes in transitional season and stages. He must stay in position being aware to be alerted of any coming danger and harm of the mother and seed.

Choosing Among Commitments

As I said before, we must be very careful choosing among commitments because it's vital to value the commitment and its preparation.

Chapter 14
False Brethren

False brethren comes with an agenda to drain and wear you out with their murmuring, complaining, self-pity, victimizing mentality. They usually come with the spirit of Azazel, also operating out of a self-centered, bitter and critical spirit. You must be very careful of them because they will come saying, its everyone else fault. They will see the wrong in everyone else life except their own. They will come with a heavy and depressive presence, attitude and dark-gloomy countenance that will saddens your whole atmosphere and environment quickly if you don't rebuke it and or separate from them.

People like this will get your pearls and use them against you to trample upon you, so be very careful what you and how much you pour into them. They need major deliverance, because if you don't deal with this spirit in the

False Brethren

beginning stage of your relationship or connection it will sabotage and shipwreck your whole ministry. They come to you as if they want help but they really don't want help their looking for strength to strengthen their agenda, justify and qualify themselves. Apostle Paul dwell with this spirit for four days following him even falsely confessing who he was outwardly but the intents of thoughts, heart and motives was wicked and had to be rebuked and addressed accordingly as should of been.

I've had false brethren come into our meetings to try to destroy, slander, steal from, accuse and try to take over the ministry and in different times I was led to deal with this spirit accordingly even putting them out. Don't let false brethren burn and wear you out.

2 Corinthians 11:26 KJV, In journeying often, in perils of waters, in perils of robbers, in perils by mine own countrymen, in perils by the heathen, in perils in the city, in perils in the wilderness, in perils in the sea, in perils among false brethren

False Brethren

2 Corinthians 11:26 NLT, I have traveled on many long journeys, I have faced danger from rivers and from robbers. I have faced dangers from my own people, the Jews, as well as from the Gentiles. I have faced danger in the cities, in the deserts, and on the seas. And I have faced danger from men who claim to be believers but are not.

Galatians 2:4 KJV, And that because of false brethren unawares brought in, who came in privily to spy out liberty which we have in Christ Jesus, that they might bring us into bondage.

Galatians 2:4-5 NLT, Even that question came up only because of some so called Christians there-false ones really-who were secretly brought in. They sneaked in to spy on us and take away the freedom we have in Christ Jesus. They wanted to enslave us and force us to follow their Jewish regulations. But we refused to give in to them for a single moment. We wanted to preserve the truth of the gospel message for you.

Chapter 15
<u>Co-Dependency</u>

Codependency means making the relationship more important to you than you are to yourself. It means you're trying to make the relationship work with someone else who's not.

Codependency is defined as a psychological condition or a relationship in which a person is controlled or manipulated by another who is affected with a pathological condition;(typically narcissism or drug addiction) and in broader terms, it refers to the dependence on the needs of, or control of another.

Codependent is define as a relationship in which one person is physically or psychologically addicted, as to alcohol or gambling, and the other person is psychologically dependent on the first in an unhealthy way.

Co-Dependency

Co-dependents people define themselves as strong enough people to deal with it when actually they need to realize that maybe they should be taking care of themselves instead of proving their strength. These people tend to stay in relationships that are unhealthy and not good for them. It's hard for these people to accept and receive compliments as well. They are the ones who start with the impression that love is sacrificial for other people, then putting up with what others wants to dish out on them to where they get deeply stuck in it.

Codependency has affected many relationships in the past and has being going on for many generations. I can attest to my codependency syndrome and codependent relationships in the past. Codependency can become a generational curse that must be broken and to where ungodly soul ties has to be severe. If this generational curse and soul ties don't be broken, cut, uprooted and destroyed even at the root of conception, it will grow from being a serpent to being a dragon to where it will pursue and chase you until it

Co-Dependency

bound you, trample upon you, overtake, overpower and destroy you. Codependency is an ENEMY BEHIND THE SCENE THAT MUST BE EXPOSE AND EXPELLED. Codependency usually stems from rejection; such as rejection from the womb that leads to self-rejection, abuse, low self-esteem, abandonment, fears of rejections, where you will began to feel unloved, unwanted, unstable, unimportant and unappreciated. Many relationships have suffered from codependency; such as ministries, marriages, friendships, parents, children, families, mentorships and etc. There were times in my life where I became co-dependent. I began to enable so many people by covering up so much which still allows them and me to remain in bondage. It took the audible voice of the Lord to speak to me and the spirit of the Lord to reveal and illuminate to me of this stronghold that held me hostage. One day several years ago after a long night of intense prayer, prophetic intercession and warfare, I was awakened and shaken literally by the voice of the Lord upon my bed, that He called my name

Co-Dependency

that woke me up and spoke CO-DEPENDENCY. It got my attention, now I had no idea what this word codependency meant but I knew the ways of my Heavenly Father, how He apprehended me and understood that He wanted me to seek out and research this. As I now sat up in my bed to listen for more I asked what this meant, then Holy Spirit revealed and illuminated the word ENABLING to me, which I knew the meaning of this word. So afterwards I began to examine myself and the people that I was in relationship with. I came to the conclusion that I was indeed enabling others addiction. I then research the word codependency and came to grips with myself that I didn't see and recognize my self-worth as I thought I done. I knew who I was in Christ Jesus as a zealot believer, daughter of Zion and woman of God that after the heart of her Father and I knew whose I were as a prophetess and wife but didn't come into agreement with whose I were as God saw me that what He had invested within me that was worth more precious than rubies that I began to waste pearls, compromise and let down my

Co-Dependency

own standards as I always taught others not to do. I began to see how the principles I taught others worked for them expediently but not me. I even began to conform to the very same things I despise which was a settlement, slave and complacent mentality. I became a slave to the strongholds of my region. I became bound by and accustomed to its climate, environment, surroundings and the people therein. I became even needy, complacent and too reliant upon those that I served under in ministry through local church membership, mentorship, association, connection and networking, to where I became an enabler of those that I served under, pastored, mentored, and was in friendship with. I begin to become overly-protective and overbearing to some, and to some I began showing false humility in ways of seeking approval of others that it even affected my marriage. I began to put others where ONLY GOD and MY HUSBAND should have been. I became an emotional wreck to where my husband watch many abused and use me because I thought he didn't understood my love but he identified it and called it out as

Co-Dependency

FALSE HUMILITY to some and ENABLED others. Through the mouths of many prophets and apostles that came to correct me personally.

People that are co-dependents and have low self-esteem are preys to this thief. People will easily misuse, mistreat and abuse you, because of your love for them and others. So if you don't come to grips with whose you are, you will get trampled upon and took advantage of. God had took about four prophets and apostles to break this spirit off of me because I didn't want to separate and let go from the relationship and under others I served. It took the Lord to come to me and tell me to stop seeking approval of others. It took the Lord to tell me that he was causing a separation and that others was going to betray and slander me badly because I didn't want to let go of the relationship when it was suppressing and oppressing me and frustrating his grace. I allowed myself to get abused and prostituted by leaders to a point I still didn't want to let go of them. God had to send a prophet from out of

Co-Dependency

North Carolina to rebuke me and cut the umbilical-cord soul ties because I didn't want to let go. He spoke of the oppression of me being the master's puppet and that God has brought it to a end. Then there came another prophetess from Atlanta Ga that told me that this was my time and that I have always put others over myself but now God wants me to put myself first and to know my own worth. She also said those dreams that I laid to the side to make other people dreams come alive, God was now going to bring my to past.

Codependency is very unhealthy and I pray you get delivered from it.

Chapter 16
<u>Growing in Wisdom</u>

The scripture says, in much wisdom comes great grief. (Ecclesiastes 1:18)

I've gotten another outlook on this scripture. Growing in wisdom is being used here interchangeably with growing in grace. In my years of ministry and relationships I've watched many come and go in my life. In fact the very ones that says that God sent them to me to help me, those that says they were sent to come under my spiritual parental care and mentorship and the ones that says I've been sent to be covenant brothers and sisters in Christ was the very ones that left me. In my many years of growing in wisdom and grace I've watched these very people that said they were sent to me to reject, betray, and abandon me. I've watched many kicked me out of their lives for their Ishmael's.

The Benefits Of Holding Onto Ishmael And Kicking Isaac Out

Many are holding onto Ishmael's and kicking Isaac's the promise unto whom God said out. I've watched many do this because they couldn't endure the discipleship training. They would then go out as a Ishmael having the same spirit as the Ishmael they're holding onto being untamed and wild attacking this same spirit the more and heaping unto themselves leaders and voices having itching ears being blown to and fro by every wind and doctrine straying away from the very truth that was imparted into them from the very beginning. I've watched these people hear my insights, instructions and warnings about coming dangers in their lives and still fall for the traps that caused them to shipwreck, have losses, become stagnant and etc. Lord knows I wanted to reach in and help but the Lord adamantly warned me to not touch it or I too will reap the same penalty and even greater.

Now that Ishmael has been planted and birthed in your vineyard among your field he/she must be circumcised, consecrated and taught as well with your household until the appointed time for you to put Ishmael and all that's connected to him out of the promise. It's imperative for you to do so. Jesus spoken in the book of Matthew and James to reinforce it saying, they were raised up together until the time of the angel of the Lord to bring about a separation. God used the same one that cause Ishmael to be planted and birth, to see the time of Ishmael ending time as was Sarah in Genesis. Time and patience has to be developing in your awaiting the promises of the Lord so you won't birth out or hold onto the Ishmael's that trying to be rooted and established in your promise. In growing in wisdom I had to realize that great grief would come with this grace especially releasing words of wisdom by watching others still get injured, bruised and discipline because of their rebuttal of my words of wisdom. Having an enlarge heart being able to see the beginning, the middle and the outcome of the person life in a particular situation is a hard thing to bear and watch but as you learn, wisdom teaches that it's not wise to try to correct a fool or they will despise you. Wisdom will also teach you that an prodigal has to learn some things through the things that they suffers and if you inherently go in to try to rescue them you will too get smite with the rod of correction. You see when a person don't gravitate towards or hold dear to wisdom as it tries to teach them, they will have to go through a time of correction and discipline to learn through experience of what wisdom tried to teach and promote them into greater place of influence. Don't allow your arrogance and stubbornness of heart to cause you to be stuck in gear, reverse or rehearse what last year lessons tried to teach you.

The Cost Of Disobedience
There have been several women that have come into my care so that I would birth them into that next place of greatness. God revealed to them through many of his languages and his ways of communicating on what to do and that I had the insights, instructions and guidance in specifics on what they need to do and go

about a situation but when they was faced with the situation it seems as if they forgotten everything that God and I said that they took another route, rejecting, abandoned and betrayed me, then paid the price of rebelling. You see it wasn't me or you that they rejected but it was the one that sent and set you into position to help advise them, so in actuality they rejected God because it was Him that gave you that wisdom and grace to release it to them to save their lives.

Why Settle???
Many of these people have settled for Ishmael's because they lost focus and hope in the promise of God because of not seeing the big picture before their eyes. Not knowing that out of the promise (Isaac) will be kings and out of Ishmael's will be princes. Why settle for a prince when you can have a king. Why settle for crumbs when you can have the whole loaf of the inheritance and blessings of the Lord. So stop verging off the path that was laid before you by trying to make yourself a way through it because you're not seeing the

results that you want to see but keep the faith and don't grow weary in well doing because you will reap if you faint not. God didn't give you that mother, father or mentor in the gospel in that season for nothing. Stop changing your mind when you don't like or agree with everything that they say because it's seem too hard for you to bear. Remember its suppose to test your character to see if you going to truly stand the test of discipleship on that level to be able to come into sonship and kingship of what the Lord has spoken. If you remember the promises of God, his instructions and why he sent you, you would value the relationship and their words dearly to your heart.

It has begun, where an individual testing in the body of Christ like never before, your spouses, your mothers or fathers won't be able to save or walk this with you. It's an individual walk alone with the Lord as He mold and shapes you for greatness, as His New Jerusalem and glorious church. Would you be able to stand the test of times as God cause a sifting, pruning, shifting, molding, and shaping in your life? Will you be able to endure the fiery furnace that's being turn up a seven times hotter?

The Good Will, The Acceptable Will And The Perfect Will

Looking at my life being a Ishmael in someone else life, also watching others plant, create, birth and hold onto Ishmael's as well in times past has caused much turmoil to their well-being and other relationships that they were in. The bible speaks of the good will, the acceptable will and the perfect will of the Lord. You will in different times of your life where you will have to be able to recognize what is the good will, the acceptable will and perfect will to know what and how much to put into the relationships, situations and places unto you feel led to go to, invest in and be a part of. However, always remember that doing something good and acceptable can even delay you or put you under the judgment of God. For example; If God gives me an specific assignment to carry out at a particular time but then I may see my brother in need of help and it seems like an emergency situation so I stop to help my brother in need and delay the instructions of the Lord because it seems like it's a good will to do and think God will accept it and that He will look over it but on the contrary this provokes the Lord to anger then now that you disobeyed the Lord you're being held under judgment. King David himself as a son, understood this and although his wife was captured he sought the Lord to see if it was time to pursue, to know when to go forth and how to go about recovering his wife, but being presumptuous thinking the Lord will look over it all the time will cause us to come under judgment even sometimes as unto death in disobedience unto the Lord as were the young prophet in 1 Kings, and King Saul. So it's vital to value the words, instructions and relationship of the Lord. The more you embrace (her) wisdom, the more grace you will gain in your administration and position in releasing wisdom.

Stepping Out On Faith, Trusting The Lord
The Lord told Abram to leave the familiar place

unto a place where the promise was, to where his name will be great. You see before Abraham was Abraham he was Abram, and God said he will make your name great. Genesis 12. This was in great detail as we see now that God was literally speaking of Abraham name as well. God will too change your name in obeying his voice. I can truly testify of this.

In 2005 before the year of my husband and I union, there came an Ishmael. God had already forewarn me of his coming before my promise comes, through much detail as dreams, visions, angelic visitation, signs, prayer, and prophecies through many vessels. Three and a half years into my budding years as a prophetess in 2005, God told me that he was sending me to Atlanta Ga where my promise land would be on assignment with much detail. Then one day I had this dream where I understood and interpreted it a little but God led me to another seer prophetess at the time to interpret it with great detail and instructions. Then in the mist of preparation to go the land of the promise with a specific assignment here comes the reality of my dream the Ishmael an old ex-boyfriend, that I tried to help lead to the Lord knowingly he was a Muslim. This Ishmael guy came in a time where I was in much persecution, slander and abandonment of my mentor, friends, family and some other members of the church. In my adamant attitude, I said I wasn't going to fall for this guy and I was too strong for it to fall now, because I had come three and a half years of purification from sex and without a man even though many had tried already to date me but this one was different.

And my dream goes:
I was in an surrounding area to that of my old house to where some guys was picking at me and tried to tear my car up because it was having problems, so I had to get out my car and walk then run because these guys picked at me, taunted me and tried to physically abuse me. I then came to this industrial factory company and by these lockers were several boys but one in particular that had on an

orange shirt caught my eye and connected to me to find where I found out his name was Frank, because he came over to talk to me. In reality Frank was a guy that I went to school with that I had a relationship with in the past in high school but ended abruptly because I relocated and was in another relationship. Back to the dream; Frank and I started talking about different things where I tried to help him as well, so afterwards I went to this museum. As I was there at the museum I begin to see there were seven to eight veils. I then begin to see behind the veils where I saw it was blue and gold, radiant shining gold especially the last veil. Then I begin to have a vision in the museum where I was translated in a open vision to Frank and his family that shown an death and grievances but I got through it. Then I came to this veil where I went beyond it and beyond it was a golden chandelier and on the lights of the chandelier was a gold ring and a gold crown that sat in different direction. On the crown and ring were the colors blue and pink. So the angels and the elders put the crown on my head but then Frank came through the crowd as the celebration and promotion went on then he got the ring down and put it on my finger but the ring was too big and didn't fit so he had to get another ring. Then I saw that a ring that fitted my finger was placed on my finger but not from Frank and then I went through this last veil the eight one with white on.

I then at this time got symbolism and interpretation from the Seer prophetess that goes as this:

-Making through the 1st few levels/stages of people picking and talking about me.
-Frank name means A Free and Shining Man.
-Museum- Historical the Past.
-Ring- Covenant. Marriage.
-Crown-Honor. Arrival. Authority. Knowledge. Wisdom.
-Veil- Stages. Levels. Something Conceal and Hidden.
-White-Purity and Faithful.
-Orange-Satanic
-7-Completion. Perfection. Maturity.

-8- New Beginnings.
-Pink means Love. Compassion. Desires
-Blue-Loyal
-She told me how the separation of the crown and ring represented that there will be a separation of me and the guy because we was going into two different directions.
-She also told me to be aware of a guy that would be from the past that was coming to try to take me back in the past but its' not going to be from God. It's only going to be an enticement of the enemy to get me to fall.

Then after this dream the same week, reality hits with persecution, slandering, people picking at me and taunting me as the dream showed, then the guy (Ishmael) from my past comes back into town to me. At first, it started off with me ministering to him, trying to get him to convert to Christianity and no longer be a Muslim but then it escalated to desiring one another. Then he moved to Atlanta Ga. Then a greater persecution came to me from the church with them not knowing anything of my ministry or involvement to this guy. To make a long story short on my birthday week still trying to endure the great persecution even at work, I received a call from him asking me to come see him in Atlanta where I got off of work earlier to do so. This was a risk I was taking because I had never driven that far before by myself, so I did. I felled this weekend. Then being in relationship with Ishmael I suffered abused of all kinds, so on the last time of me and the guy his nephew dies as was shown to me in the dream above to where I went back to Atlanta to get him and this time his homeboy went with me to pick him up. I let this Ishmael guy get to comfortable my settling for him because he began do drug trafficking in my car speeding 100 mph knowing good and well I had an expired tag on my car and no insurance. Going to get him me and his home boy, we was almost ran off the road going across the bridge of Oconee Lake by some 18 wheelers being in front of me, beside me and two behind me as I was driving. I begin to cry out to the Lord at this time with my life flash before my eyes. This was the last weekend me and the guy spent together. In the mist of me and his intimacy I stopped him, burst out in tears crying out to God in repentance and said I am disappointing my God. I then took him back home from the funeral later that day. Then that following week, our church had it annual conference with the guest speaker Bishop Neil Ellis to where I felt he preached my entire situation and then he said it was someone in here that has gotten in a situation but don't know how to get out of it but want too then said God says when you wake up the next morning, say This is the day the Lord has made now lay it on me Lord. I blessed God for my answer and prayed the more that night and followed instructions that morning, then the guy called about 3 hours afterwards and told me he had just got into it with his family and that he was packing to move back to Delaware. He asked me to come to see him and wait for him but I broke it off that day and said to him by next year this time I will have met my husband to be that God sends me and sure enough it happened as I spoken it prophetically. My God I thank you for your sovereignty. That next year I ran into my God sent husband doing the work of the Lord in the church that I was sent to where I ministered through song and where me and my friend help do deliverance there by helping to cast demons out and help others receive the gift of the holy spirit with the evidence of speaking in tongues. How God done it was awesome.

Although I felled for Ishmael and felt ashamed by my falling it still worked out for my good, because I got back into position but with greater respect, fervency, boldness, faith, confidence and wisdom of the Lord that it caused me to start seeking out the land of Atlanta by myself as God said before the Ishmael came and then later on in the beginning on the next year I moved to Atlanta Ga in February of 2006 with the blessing and counsel of my apostle where later that year in the eight month in August in the ending of my assignment of Atlanta me and my husband the Isaac the king my promise our journey began. Now me and my husband is back into the land of the promise as God moved us up here last year in 2013 but I will touch on some of that too but by now you can see the fulfillment of my dream and why I elaborated so much on it.

Letting Go Of The Old

You see holding onto old connections, people, places and things will hinder you from prospering. Its unfruitful holding onto such things and people that God has told you to let go, because you will remain stagnate, become sluggish and be delayed in moving forth into the promise and destiny in momentum. How can you truly embrace the newness such as the new and best wine holding on to the old? You can't do it, it can't be done. New wine will never be able to be contained and preserved into old bottles. You will have to let go of the old and the counterfeit (Ishmael) so you can truly enjoy the promises of the Lord. So remember that New wine skins has to be formed, so this will cause you to have to let go and let God dismantle the old mantle and remove the old people so that the Isaac's could come forth.

Testing Of Character

Let's examine the life of Abraham and Sarah. Genesis 15. When God sends a Sarah into your life it's only to bless you. Sarah was a midwife that desired to have a natural baby of her own. She was given the name Sarah before she even became a natural mother because she was already a spiritual mother, mother of Zion and mother of many nations. She gave birth to too many women by helping them in their conception and delivery. God change the name and dismantled Sara so that Sarah the mother of many nations to come forth. You see as she was giving birth to others and helping others in their time of birth, she was too giving birth to her promise and greater leader as well. Sara was held into captivity in Egypt for a while where she found the bond woman Hagar. Sara was presumptuous, rashly in her actions because of weariness, taunting desires, impatience and dishearten in heart. She acted hasty by inquiring Hagar to lay with her husband and conceive a child then influenced her husband to lay with Hagar (bondwoman) that gave life to a counterfeit.

Growing in Wisdom

Although the bondwoman son had entitlement and gain inheritance, he still wasn't the chosen one to receive the birthright and whole lump of the benefits and inheritance of the promises. In Sarai watching the pregnancy and hearing the taunting remarks of the bondwoman she became dishearten where she became overbearing that drove Hagar away but the angel met Hagar, blessed her seed then instructed her back to serve up under the mentorship and covering of Sarai. No matter how hard the mentorship, covering, parental guidance was Hagar was sent back to endure it to make sure she gave birth to a healthy baby. Many times it become a challenge to be under the tutelage of a hard leader but sometimes its' all for the making of your character. Then later on Sarai saw again how Ishmael began to mock Isaac and said this is going to be a problem. Sarah saw what happened to her with Hagar before when she was pregnant and now it was happening to her through the children and saw how this was going to affect the inheritance. You see in every level and stage of life there's an promise that is fulfill, there's an enemy that must be expelled, overthrown and uprooted, there's a giant that must be conquered and battle to be won. Sarah began to see this of what Ishmael was doing to Isaac knowing that this wasn't just her own frustrations, desires or jealousy but she felt and saw what the Lord felt and seen as a hindrance to the fulfillment of the promises of God.

As we saw with Sarah we too see with Abraham being hasty in his sayings and disheartens when speaking with the Lord saying that Eleazar an outcast will be his heir that inherits it all. Why are we trying to give outcast, bondwomen and their sons the promise portion? I say to you remain faithful, loyal and consistent in your waiting because you will reap if you faint not.

Let me share another testimony of me and my husband journey coincide Abraham and Sarah journey coming into the promise land although all promises are not yet fulfilled. God revealed

Growing in Wisdom

the more to me on the Daybreak of this February 22, 2014. Here goes:

The Lord told Abraham to bring him a three year old heifer, female goat, ram, turtledove and pigeon. Three years and 11 months we have been overseers/pastors in ministry. House of Refuge International was launched out by leaving our former father in the gospel house by faith to start House of Refuge in April 22, 2010. We obeyed the Lord even though others didn't understand it. We endure hardships and great persecution of former leaders, we went through droughts and famines, where many abandoned, attacked, betrayed and denied us but we stood with the strength of our Lord God and the new divine connection and governance (our father and mother in the gospel) where we had met prior to being launched out from the ministry. You see through my four years of being a budding prophetess in the first ministry I didn't want to let go of the ministry and the leaders even after the overbearing and jezebelic ways and tendencies of my former mentor, I too was instructed back under her care for a time in ministry as was Hagar. I couldn't leave when I wanted to go because of being hurt. I had to conquer the giant and that stage of my journey as a making prophetess. I had to complete my assignment in the lives of others and get my blessing as the young prophetess being on assignment into going into my seasonal stage as a prophetess. I valued the church I was in and the leaders I was under and although I felt unfairly mistreated I still didn't want to go even when God told me to go. So it cause the Lord to push me out of my comfort zone literally by burning down my house to get me to go on ahead to Atlanta Ga where he told me to go and the only thing he told me when I cried out to him on February 14 2006 in the middle of the night, in an desolate apartment with no electricity, no nothing but I cried and travailed until daybreak then and the only thing the Lord showed me through a night vision was a pocket that had the word push on it so then I gave up my will and went on to Atlanta Ga area to Stone Mountain Georgia where I went to an apartment complex that gave me favor with giving me an apartment with no money down. I valued my relationship with my church that much that it took the storm of the Lord to uproot me in such a away because I didn't want to let go of the old for my promise, knowing my husband was awaiting and needed me in this time of moving forward. How many of you delaying your spouse's arrival, because you don't want to let go of the old ways and comfort zone.

Learning To Let Go
Now back to me and my husband launching out in going forth with the ministry God told us to go forth in. Before we launched out, God had told us like a year before that we was to go forth in our own ministry through many confirmations in great details but because we valued the relationship with our local church, we didn't won't to step out and even leave them. We serve faithfully in ministry there being in leadership as well as seasoned leaders. We were one of our pastors right arm laborers, sons and daughters in the ministry, so you know it was hard. I loved my mother in

the gospel so much and fought for her tremendously against many that tried to rebuttal against her but then when God himself came to us and shared with us about the separation we fought against it. We even fought against the negative things we heard and saw that being spoken and done against us as God shared. Then this one day when I was in prayer and prophetic intercession I was visited by the tangible presence of the Lord in my living room where there I seen the heavens opened and through this portal many angels came down from this latter into my room, surrounded and accompanied me but before they was release to move, assist me and operate the Lord spoke to me about that was coming. He said a sword of division was coming that will divide us from the ministry and to be of good courage in the mist of the storm and great persecution and that he was sending my midwives angels to help me give birth to this great baby and that I needed assistance in giving birth to it and then as the Lord continued talking I saw how the angels filled the room stood hovering around me and when he was through talking they assisted me in giving spiritual birth as I prayed and travailed fervently in groaning's as the spirit of the Lord gave me utterance in a fetus position bared down literally up against my wall, sweating tremendously then angels left the room. After this night all that the Lord had revealed came into existence, persecution from every angle in ministry hit hard at us from the head on down but I knew our angels was assisting us because I could see them and even see them as many shining flickers and lightning bolts. We was attacked on every angle and called everything except for being a child of God. One day me and my husband visited my old ministry to where an apostle from North Carolina was a guest speaker, he called me up and told me how that was angels that was accompanying me but he saw a huge angel standing hovering over me to make sure I was protected and that destiny and my words would be carried out. Then he called my husband out and told him that someone missed their blessing because they didn't want to step in place so God was going to give him there's and the one that was already destine for him. After that many ran to us even during this time that wanted leave the ministry but we advise them strongly not to do so and that they was needed there to help the man and woman of God and to finish with their own development but some of those very ones went back slandered and lied on us. Even in all of this we continue to stay in the ministry even after all of this persecution in ministry but then the Lord sent the very guest speakers that our pastor had down for a revivals at the time prophesying to us about our time was up and to our pastor to release and embrace us or God want going to take us away from him. The very same words that we spoke to our pastors about how to build the ministry, was what the guest speakers spoke to them. This happened many times. Then one day when our church was having a another revival our pastors overseer brought a apostolic team with her and one of the prophets that with her, I had already met once before while traveling with her and assisting her in planting and building another church in another region. This prophet that was with her came to me after the service that night and told me around another leader and said to me very sternly but compassionately that they are using me and that I was like their master puppet doing and moving to everything they say as they want with me even knowing their heart towards me, I still desire to serve. Then he says but God says he comes to severe the ties tonight, cut the umbilical cord that I will no longer let them use me again and that I will be free to go forth in the work of the Lord that God was calling me to start now. This prophet of the Lord was from California that was visiting with our overseer cried as he spoke these words to me. He said he saw my tears, faithfulness and hard labor but they still wasn't giving honor but stealing, abusing and using me up but God is removing me now from them. I told my husband what was spoken to me as well as the other leader did, because my husband had to work that night and I had to lead praise and worship. Telling my husband all of this he began to get a better sense of awareness of the ending work in the ministry there but he still needed more confirmation because he loved his pastor more than anything and wanting make sure his work was carried out. Then the Lord began to show him through visions, dreams, prayer, sent prophets and apostles down from all parts of the world to confirm his call the more and that this was the will of the Lord to start this new work of our own. We both was invited to three apostles houses in Carolina that was in covenant with our apostle and they shared with us that God as well told them that it was our time to go and gave us some words of wisdom and guidance and build structure how to do so in planting and building the Lord work. Even after this we still didn't leave the ministry but my husband gravitating more towards my pastors and neglected me for a time even came against me because he didn't see how serious this was or better yet he didn't want to let go. You see the Lord knew that I was going to get persecution, rejected and abandonment even in my own home and this was the need of the assisting in the visitation of the angels. He knew that it would take more for my husband to have to come into agreement with his plan and will, than it did me because this was his church and pastor that he had served from the beginning and longer than I did. I had been through this in ministry before but God sent more prophets and apostles to confirm what he had already spoken to me and him but the last prophetess that spoken to him penetrated and had no knowledge or connection to our apostle for my husband to come into alignment with the will of the Lord, although we both still didn't want to let going all of the hell we was going through, we did. My husband went to our apostle where they had a meeting and told him that God had call out to start our own word and if he could have his blessing but even if he didn't get the blessing he still had to obey the Lord this time. You see how we are with valuing relationships so much it has to take the Lord to come in to tear us apart. We believe in covenant keeping but in our valuing we had to grow in wisdom in learning how to let go when God say to let go. Now God is restoring unto us the joy of our salvation in House of Refuge as well as our personal life. He have sent us to the land that was promised.

Opposition Into Transitioning Into The Promise Land

The first week of us being here in the Atlanta Ga area in Covington Ga we was headed to an interview that my husband scheduled for but when we call to find out more details of location they said he had to have more paperwork and that they had to postpone his interview and someone said he was in the system. Yes they gave him a run around. So that whole week he and I put in job applications but nothing wasn't coming through until the next week on a Monday where I awakened from a prophetic dream that follows exactly what about to happen next. I received a phone call from a daycare job. They asked me would I come in for an interview that day. As we was headed to my job interview we came into the city limits where a sign read "Welcome, you have now entered into the land of the Promise" we couldn't believe what we saw, we was amazed and ecstatic by the confirmation and blessings of our Covenant God. You see in Abram trying to fulfill the call of God on his life by trying to establish ministry, he came to a drought and famine in wilderness as was I before I met my husband and as was me and my husband together trying to go forth in ministry and into the promise land of the Lord. Abram came to a famine where his wife Sarai was held into captivity in Egypt by Ambilech as I was held into jail on this same day I went to my interview, got the job but had to go get a criminal background check where I found out I had a violation probation warrant for expired tag out for my arrest in the August because of a debt that I owe from 2006. We were trying to get establish into the Land of the promise after seeing the sign I stated earlier. As I was held into captivity my husband was praying but yet going through hardships here in the land but more hurdles and roadblocks came against him. He pushed and pressed inspite all of it to where God still opened doors for work for him when naysayers fought and accuse him and abandon him, to where he got kick out of a house to get a motel with the little money he had to stay at until my release day out of jail. We came to Atlanta on faith with about four hundred dollars awaiting my husband last check from that Friday from his other job and awaiting more money to come from the government but it didn't come until my exact release day out of jail. God had already told me in Jail that He bought me into bondage without money and that He was going to be release me out without money. My husband tried his best to gather money to get me out of jail even on a bond which was seven hundred dollars but God wouldn't allow it from no one. He asked many people to help him but God made a way that no one could get me out because there was truly a need for me to be held into captivity. God told me, he led me into captivity to hold captivity captive. I had a specific assignment there that had to be fulfilled where I am completing my book on my experiences and journey of being held in jail in captivity. Many didn't understand the method of the Lord and why this time to do such a thing that it even looked bad on us but God it was all for purpose. In my incarcerated time I ministered to many whereas to a woman of God that served me and was mentored by me was released the next day I was released, and a caucasian pregnant woman that was my first cellmate was released on the same day as I was, as Hagar the bondwoman was released with Sarai in her release time along with the monies of provision. I recognized this and also saw how God wouldn't let the bondwoman stay in the land no longer than two weeks in my land after we provided for her naturally and spiritually in our area/land but then she moved back home to New York but we still stay in contact. You see when Ambilech released Sarai back unto Abram he didn't released to him her with her hands empty but she brought them restoration and restitution. The day I was released I wasn't released empty handed but there were a young eight month pregnant woman that was my cellmate bunkey left the same day as I and there was another woman that served me in there leaving the next day, also the government released the money that was held up and due us then we got an increase of more money and my husband got his job check on the same day. You see the Isaac sowed and reap in the same year.

Growing in Wisdom

When I got out of incarceration we was riding around one day in our city and lo and behold a sign caught my attention and my husband and the woman of God that driving conversing but God got my attention and told me to look at this sign that was the city limit sign as I have looked at it before but under the sign is what I never paid attention to that God wanted me to see was another sign that said You have now entered into the city of Excellence. Now you know I'm like Lord why are you showing the signs first? I asked everybody that was in the car did they see the sign and they said no .I told them what it said and the young lady that was driving said that a lie about the city and they are nowhere near excellence because she stayed here for some years now. I then thought of myself of what God was saying about the region temperament, where it needs to come up to, why we was sent here and even ourselves taking upon the spirit of excellence. So I asking myself again why am I the only one seeing these signs first? God spoke and revealed to me that because he promised me back in 2005, nine years ago about the promise land He would bring me back to. Even the Lord revealed how he had to drive out some people that was still in our lives from the past that was in our land before we came and if we was to come any time before it would have been worst so he had to weed them out. God had to get rid of Ishmael's as he did before with the guy that came before my husband. Now you see even when Ishmael's was planted and birth it still caused me to seek out our promise land, pursue harder the Lord and destiny, see what I didn't want nor need to where I came into a famine that caused me to birth out and meet my promise Kerenski Usry where we are now here together pressing towards destiny watching the Lord order our steps. Sarai job was to be a midwife and a mother of the nations as is mines. Sarai brought increase to her household working and laboring in her own house among her own people and peers, as is mines. I've tried many times to get a nine to five job in my wanting help my husband bring in income to the house but every time I've been close to getting a job to even getting hired a prophet of the Lord out the blue along with the Lord telling me and my husband himself and roadblocks that will come to stop the getting hired now on someone else job. I've been ridiculed and scoffed at by family especially because of not having a nine to five job but God didn't put that in me to job settle or better yet get comfortable on job because every job that I've had have while been married have been seasonal job that didn't last longer than a year. All my jobs have been as an assignment where I too gain and learn the business side of things to establish and build my own business. Why settle for a prince nation like Ishmael when you came become a king and ruler like Isaac.

You see Sarai was called by God to be a midwife, where she instructed and was covered by her husband to stay dedicated in her own field no matter what others around her thought, gave birth to, done, prospered in or said . This was for myself as well. My life and mantle have shifted to not only just being a prophetess but being a mother of Nations because I valued the relationship I was in and valued me and the Lord relationship more as where I grew in wisdom and grace. Becoming a mother that is a wife, prophetess, and woman of God that walks in wisdom assisting other mothers before conception, during pregnancy and after birth I take joy in seeing many lives being transform before my eyes. You see I had to conquer another place in life where I didn't give wisdom out and judge cases but I had to be able to grow and walk in wisdom myself through experiences by being in the school of the Holy Spirit. Holy Spirit crushed the oil out of me on a whole another level. Isaiah 60. Now because of this birthing place I now can show others that's in leadership how to overcome such obstacles and mother their flock as I've done by growing in grace and wisdom of the Lord.

Accurately Defining Your Relationship

It's vital to define in the beginning what the purpose of the person that has come into your life, because if you don't you want know the value and you will also begin to give too much, too little when you suppose to tread careful and give just a little swine and people that are just came to spectate or for a season but to the ones its supposed to be more personal as Jesus himself demonstrated to us. In every relationship there is freedom but there also boundaries to how much and far you can go with a person. It's also wise to discern the level of maturity the person is and their strengths and weaknesses. Know who your Ishmaels, you Isaacs, your John Marks, Your Gehazi's, your Elijah's, your Joshua's, your Timothy, your Peter's, your Judas's, your Ruth's and your John's. My years of growing in wisdom and grace I has to be able to recognize this and tried to establish but some didn't accept the demand of maturity on the relationship. I began to see the hearts many that said they was for me but actually was swines and stray dogs. After my time of being incarcerated some old friends and mentorees began to attack me as God had already reveal but God sent 3 different apostles and prophets that didn't have knowledge of the situation to tell me it was time to let them go, this apostle name that season for me and said it's wise to

Growing in Wisdom

accurately define your relationships in this season and it rung in my spirit then the next day when a old friend begin to attack me for no cause God gave me a babysitter job and while the old constantly inbox and texted me God spoke to me why he gave me that job in the mist of that situation then he said to me adamantly and strongly to stop babysitting grown folks and as I elaborated on that word I heard in my spirit again stop babysitting grow folks for free your pearls and time are valuable and very precious. God will use the foolish things to confound the wise. When God said this to me it was sudden rushing wind came strong over me in the kitchen fixing the kids food and the wind came with so much joy and laughter that it brought much freedom and release. The way God uses me and speak me is also through natural things and circumstances and you're in an situation such as when I was with the women constant rebuttal and accusations through text God caused me to gain more wisdom and grace in the situation. God know I had wrestled with those spirits in those individuals for seven years straight and there years being in my life had come to an end.

When Joseph was put in prison he met two your men and they were as the Butler and the Baker. Then one day both told their dreams to Joseph the Butler dream was stating that within three days he was would regain his freedom by being repositioned back into position where he got a promotion as well. The Baker dream revealed that in three days that his time had to come to an end where his head would be cut off. When I was in jail I literally went through a similar situation where me, a young lady and two guys was in the holding cell to go before the judge. Both of the young men being in a different holding from me and the young woman right next to us began to share their situation and life to me. One young man began to complain and say that it was his first time being in jail but the other young man said that he stays back in forward in jail. I listened to the attitudes of the young men and all they shared with me and the young woman then I ministered to them.

Growing in Wisdom

Then God reveal to me about Apostle Paul and Silas being in jail as well as Joseph them scenario. I then told the young lady about the story of Apostle Paul and Silas and said lets praise and worship the Lord and we did. Then the young man that I constantly stayed in jail told me he felt something turn in him where he began to purge and then praise God as and encourage the other young man praise the Lord with us but he wouldn't I then began to encourage the young through song of the Lord but he stayed focus on his situation but the other young began to surrender out Loud to the Lord and then the guards came from the back and got the young man that it was his first time. The other young man began to tell me he thank me and knew I was a preacher and began to confess to me about all his wrongs of what he done in life the more although I listened I directed him to give all to the Lord and ask God into his life and he did and we all prayed for the other young that was very discourage still but then continue to praise and worship the Lord and then the guards brought the other young man back into the cell as he was even more saddened where he told us they gave him 30 years in prison or pay 30,000 and he said it was no one he had to get him out. Then the guards came and got the other guy. The other guy went out rejoicing in the name of Jesus as we now felt bad for the other guy trying to encourage him to more. Then the guards brought the other guy out and he rejoice when he came out and told us that they release him to go home and then the judge gave him a job with him. Then he said this what being under the power of the blood of Jesus would do for you if you just trust him and give it all to him. Look at God.

This was prime examples of the Butler and Baker. The Butler representing the new wine and newness while the Baker represented the old wine, false burdens, dead weight, dismantling being in the pit. The Butler interceded and help usher in the deliverer Joseph to feet of the Pharoah to deliver and preserve the land in the time of famine and plenty. The Butler was reposition back into position as the Butler but this time serving a better wine as it was with my life in the situation with the two women that I mentioned earlier. After being release from jail a month later the two women attacked me then God literally sent a prophet to speak to me that released a rhema word to cut off them and where God was taking to me to greater and higher place and the prophet name was Butler as sign to my situation. Ain't God good? God revealed the Butler situation to me in different aspect then release the Baker aspect as well. The baker aspect was how the baker dream as he revealed to Joseph about how he saw the black birds pecking and attacking his head with the basket on it. As God revealed to me my situation in this situation he showed how the blacks birds was these same women that went through these same cycles that began to constantly attack my head which is my headship and authoritative place. Therefore their season and time had come to completion and to an end in my life, so I had to die to the desires of holding on to them being in my life as well as they had to die to the desires me being in their life. God then began to remind me of the dreams he had given me that following that same week exactly what they would and was saying who they was backbiting with and who they would seduce in helping them to try to defeat me. God also show me that week how the black birds was trying to come challenge, confront and cut off the heads of the eagles and doves. Then Holy Spirit reminded me of the instructions and dreams of instructions and cutting off I had to do with them as well as with some others that included an tornado separating me from them because I still wanted to help them and didn't want to let go because I valued our relationships so much. In the middle of February 2014 where the earth began to groan and shift where there was many season change in one week. There was snow one day, rain one day, summer and heat one day, earthquake one day and then a tornado watch and warning one day all in Georgia. This terrified many but I sought the Lord about it knowing there was never a time like this. I was living in a small town and knowing our state wasn't prepared for that, especially not a earthquake. God began to show me where me and my husband was in our season and our we had to dissociate ourselves with someone people as I woke one the beginning of February with God audibly spoke to me and told me it was time for me to disassociate from someone in this particular season because of their prideful, stubborn, and rebellious ways. God release me to remind them of things and dreams and words he had already spoken to them, he gave me instructions through words of wisdom before, during and after but they still remained to humble themselves, then He openly exposed and rebuked them through 3 other people but they still remain to yield so He told me to disassociate myself and remained me of the tornado dream and that their was a couple more that will be separated from me that was full of pride and religious ways. It really took alot for me to separate at this time because this relationship was a year old year and we had just really began to grow as they said the Lord told them I was their midwife but I tried to help them as much as I could but God told me I had to pull back for a time. Yes I was

Growing in Wisdom

growing more in wisdom and grace and this time I was determine to pass the test that God said I was taking to get to this greater place and I was guarding this with everything I had because I wanted to pass this test as God show me through my dream the I took and made a 100 on it and had the highest GPA in the school. I was determined to pass therefore I had to allow this time wisdom to lead me and I follow.

You see during your testing time all types of things will come to test and tempt you but who will you answer to and who will you resist? God showed me through a dream last week about some sharp shooters hidden behind a tree being ordered by this woman that seduce and trick this man to sell his soul and everything he had to her and then ordered him to kill some people, then she had then order this other guy behind him to make sure he get the job done and if not kill him along with some others. So the guy that sold his soul and possessions returned to the place where he made the pat with her as I watched in my car from a distance, then I began to see his countenance become sadden and dull and said that to himself he couldn't do it. So I began to open the door to get out the car to go to the man to encourage him but then I saw a she lion head towards his way to him but then wicked woman came out of the woods and confronted him and then destroyed him.

In my seeing this in the dream I woke up with the dream being very upon my heart as I sought the Lord on it and then I got revelation concerning it and said the Thief, Killer and Destroyer. Then I prophetically spoke the killer doesn't have nothing on or not as powerful as the Thief and the Destroyer. More scriptures came to my spirit where I thought of they may kill this body but they can't cause my soul to be destroyed. The thief will come to rob you of your identity, inheritance and possession in the Kingdom of God and then destroy your soul but I refuse to let him do that to me nor the people that I'm connected to. About thirty minutes after waking up from that dream we receive a phone call from another old leader that had bad worldly issues where he left a message and this was a time God told me don't answer and to be careful of him as I thought of the dream. Now we must move with and sensitive to the timing of God because distractions is trying its way to seduce you so you want have the fulfillment of the promises of God. This is not for you to get paranoid but to stay prayer and watchful that you will be able to discern the times when God want you to move and answer the call or resist the temptations, because in your accelerated place many will come to deceive you but stay in that to be able to discern the voices, seasons and times.

If you haven't done so already began to define the relationship and recognize the purpose as to why you're place in someone life and why they're yours because the devouring lion study you to steal, kill and destroy you. The black birds ready to snatch your seed and sabotage the promises right before you're about to give birth to it as they tried to do with Abraham in Genesis 15:11. In September of 2010 a prophet from Ghana Africa came down right after our ordination and persecution time. he then called me out into the aisle, told me and my husband to come to the front and told me that he saw a black birds around my womb/stomach and saw how every time I'm at my peak about to give birth or try to conceive that the black birds will come and snatch it but God comes to reveal to redeem he says. He began to go on to me and my husband about how the enemy will try to come stop us from having a natural baby but God will give us a baby. H has elaborated about the apostolic call on my husband life and how strong the prophetic grace was upon my life but he told me how I had to let go some people in my life and release them out of my spirit and that the very same people that I pour my life out to and give my all is the people began turn on me and work against me and he also elaborated on the way God made me, my heart and have me to release even hard sayings is that many was going to be offended but blessed that not offended because of me says the Lord. Last weekend February 22, 2014 I began to have bad stomach cramps and so my husband came to pray for me and run my stomach and I went to sleep until about 2:30am I woke up and my husband went to sleep then. Then as soon as he went to sleep around 2:45-3:30am in the morning I began to have bad cramps in my stomach again but didn't want to awake my love. Then I begin speaking in my heavenly language and God spoke to me it shall come forth and I will chased away the black birds the vultures, carcasses that tried to come to steal my seed again. I then was in the bathroom and enlighten that I was now about to give birth and what I was experiencing an in between the times of contractions and attacks, so I began to get aggressive in warfare by binding up hindrances and constipation, breaking barrenness off my womb, unstopping wells and chasing away the black birds that came against me and at this time as I was warring I was sitting on the toilet with the bible in right hand and my left hand on my stomach. After I bind up, broke, broke the powers and chased away, I loosed my bile's to come into alignment that my bowel will move and my organs to come into alignment, released the wells to spring forth like never before, prophesied to life to my womb and call forth the promises into existence with a little more elaborations but you get where I'm going and after those prophetic prayers no longer than two minutes I broke free, purged, bowel moved, stomach began to move, deliverance came. I then moved to the living-room rejoicing in the Lord of his goodness. Then I sat down thought about how my Abraham, my protector my husband had already covered, prayed over me and spoke life to my womb then he Let God be God by taking care of me as I rested so peacefully then I arose as God then put him to sleep to be with me the more. Oh how I love the Lord.

Identifying My Season

As I sat now on my sofa I thought of how the enemy fought the coming together of the new divine connection that was going to take place later that day when we meet with some new prophets friends. I then sat there and meditated on the goodness of the Lord, but then Holy Spirit begin to reveal Abraham and Sarah situation to me where He instructed me to go study Abraham again. In my time of in depth study and more prayer God revealed more. I got lost in seeking God and study to where I got alarmed in my spirit of the season and time, then I heard and the DAYBREAK'S. I then looked at the window and saw the coming of the day as Holy Spirit spoke to me and said God changed your name. I rejoiced, spoke it loud and said "God change my name, God change our names". I will never be the same again Glory to our Great God!

In Genesis 15:12-23. You see the Lord shown Abram the future of the enslaved nations of his people but he also showed him the coming deliverer that will persevered them Joseph his great grandson and the deliverer that will deliver them out of bondage Moses. Abram gain a greater prophetic lenses and scope to be able to see further into four generations down into the future where the his people was enslaved 400 years, along with God telling him that he will live a long life and how his own death will be. Oh how awesome God is and the prophetic.

As God done with Abram, He also done with me at this time. He begin to lengthen my prophetic scope and lenses in comparison with the life of Abram and Sarai. Then continue to elaborate as read. In Genesis 16:4-6, Hagar begin to mocked, ridicule and treat Sarai her mother in the Gospel and midwife with contempt, that it grieved Sarai because she was barren at the time. There comes a time in life where you would have those ones treat you as Hagar treated Sarai. Mother's will get out of order, mocked, rebuttal, rebel and treat their midwives and leaders with contempt because they don't see them with natural things or natural things happening in their life where it will seem to them that you're unfruitful but not. In this time the Lord will show whose wrong and whose right by judging between the two as he's done through my life on many occasions. Sarai then felt very dishearten where she took this matter to her husband Abram and he insisted her to do what she will with her but

Growing in Wisdom

Sarai took advantage of the instructions and advice of her husband by retaliating where she began to become overbearing, dominating, enslaving and mistreat Hagar to where Hagar fled. Oh how we all can testify to this situation. In Hagar attempt to flee being pregnant she was met by the angel of the Lord being one of the first women to have an encounter of the Lord where then release the word of the Lord. Yes she prophesied! The angel of the Lord told Hagar to return to her mother/midwife and submit herself back under her authority although the retaliation of what Sarai done to her. You God will guide you right back under your leader that you felt done you wrong as he done here in the old testament and new testament and as I said he done to me earlier. Yes it maybe hard, difficult or challenging but it's all worthy. You will see the valuables in it at the end until your time of separation, releasement and birthing comes but until them stay put because it's all for the making of your character and health of your baby you're carrying.

After the angel instructed her back he then blessed her Hagar womb of the baby that she carried and name he by the name which is Ishmael, meaning God hears in the time of your distress. Now in the seasons to where God allows Ishmael to be planted and birthed because of your impatience, He will still bless them by raising them up as a great nation as well but still separate you from them and show you how much to pour into and how much to give Ishmael. The angel further on to say that this son of yours that you're carrying, will be wild and untamed as a donkey. He will raise his fist against everyone and everyone will be against him. Yes he will live in open hostility against all his relatives. Now we see the characteristics of a Ishmael type as the angel of the defined him.

Characteristics Of Spirit Of Ishmael
When you come into contact with an Ishmael they will normally be wild and untamed, meaning being unteachable, resentful, wild and free spirited going from one place to another. Looking for establishment. Prideful.

Haughty. Aggressive. Adamant. Hostile. Rebellious. Have itching ears. Presumptuous. Spiteful. Divisive. Unstable. Double-minded. Schizophrenic. Rejected. Resentful. Disloyal. Outcasts. Abused. Enslaved. Galatians 4:21-31.

In Hagar attempt to flee from her mistress Sarai she was met by the angel of the Lord that bless her womb and her son that she carried and also instructed her back subjected to Sarai. In angel speaking to her she then return with a prophecy unto the Lord that said You are the God that sees me and in that place her wilderness and deserted place at the well was marked and named Beerlahairoi meaning Wells of the living One who sees me.

Identifying And Establishing Covenant

Thirteen years passed Abraham being 86 to 99 years old when God came back to him as Elshaddi, God Almighty. He spoke to Abraham saying, serve me faithfully and lived a blameless life. God changed their names from Abram to Abraham and Sarai to Sarah and blessed them extremely fruitful, then he told Abraham that he will confirm his covenant with him. As I stated earlier that God spoke to as well and I change your name when it was at daybreak and as he also told Abraham that he would confirm his covenant with he done so even later on that day with us although we know there's a continuation of confirming the covenant. God confirms his covenant with Abraham through angelic visitation to Abraham and Sarah a year later about her being pregnant with the promise son. Now you can truly see the similarity with our lives being compared to Abraham and Sarah. God has promised us a son and daughter plus he has given us names for them. Oh how this brings comfort, joy and encouragement to my heart and I hope it does to yours. However, the natural son wasn't the only promise that God made with Abraham but he made a covenant concerning his spiritual children, his name would be forever remembered, his legacy, the everlasting promises of the many generations to come about how God will continue be with

his people and bring deliverance to them.
Genesis 17.

Understanding The Valuables Of Covenant
Further on in communication with the Lord
Abraham goes on to ask God about Ishmael.
Look at the heart of a father's love to consider
all his children in the blessings. Truly he was a
man the value the relationships that God gave
him and was connected to. So Abraham asked
the Lord could Ishmael live under the special
covenant and special blessings but God said
No! He couldn't live under the special
covenant. Many of you may not agree with this
next statement of what I'm to say but I believe
it to be true. Many of you have gotten children
outside of or before your covenant marriage
that would not be getting the covenant
blessing. You see our God is a covenant
keeper by whole lots of value to it for anyone
to come to abort or break it. Although God is a
God of no respect of persons however He is a
God that is a respect of principles and holds
value to covenant. God watches over His
words to perform them making sure they come

to pass because He is not a man that He shall lie nor the Son of Man to repent. There are times when a man has gotten an children outside of his covenant marriage and God will purposely cause a diversion to have that child to be put out of the household to sustain the promises and to make sure that nothing comes to abort that or undermined that plan. Some will not understand this plan and even wants to stone you because it seems as if you have neglected, abandoned or rejected the other child/children but the will of God sometimes is not quite understanding but it's to be carried out.

However, in this time of the promise son and blessings, God will not leave nor abandon the other son but on the contrary bless him as well as He shared with Abraham in their time of conversing. God said to Abraham that Ishmael will be blessed also, just as He have asked and even said before. That He will make Ishmael extremely fruitful and multiply his descendants. That he will become a father of 12 princes, and that he will make him a great nation a well. Gen 17:19-20. In Abraham and Sarah house shall be 12 kings (Isaac's). In Abraham's and Hagar's house shall be 12 princes (Ishmael's). Isaac representing The Covenant and Ishmael representing the Connection.

Learning To Let Go

God told Abraham about this time next year that Sarah will conceive which will make 14 years passed. Being in in depth on this God gave me an in depth prophetic insight on the ministry of me and my husband and the ministry we established in our hometown Jefferson County Georgia and the promise land Atlanta Ga. He spoke in depth concerning House of Refuge (our ministry name) Jefferson County and House of Refuge Atlanta Ga and how House of Refuge International will rebirth in 2014. Look at the significant numbers in this. The numbers 3 and 4 and the numbers 13 and 14. God made covenant with Abraham 13 years later and gave him instructions to circumcise everyone with when Ishmael was 13 years old. The numbers 13 is emphasis here. In the year of 2013 many things happened in our lives. There were a circumcision and consecration that came to the House of Refuge Jefferson County where we celebrated our Third as a ministry. In this same year there were a circumcision where all left us and the many ended as God had already shared with us and the ministry in Jefferson County that if they didn't honor the gifts which was us that God had given to them that God was going to send them to the land where they will receive the honor in the Land of the promise. So House of Refuge Jefferson County came to an end. We then relocated to the Atlanta area. I went to jail and as I was incarcerated my husband was going through circumcision as well as completed the ending work in Jefferson County and coming to grips that this baby has ran its course and was it a hard thing to end this work here.

You see House of Refuge was basically raised up in the wilderness where we had services in our home and in a member home in the beginning stages where both homes was way out in the woods. God sent us people that were in transition, that was hurt, broken, wounded, wild, outcast, rejects, yet loving, intelligent and bold that needed deliverance and inner healing. God sent many of them to the House of Refuge Jefferson County from different states and cities such as Michigan, Miami, Carolina, and Georgia. Lord knows we valued this work and the people that came and was sent to us and we didn't want to let this work go but God said the time had come that the work was completed. When I think of them even now I get moved with compassion inside because I love them dearly and have prayed that none be lost. 14 years later God visited Abraham and Sarah then she was with child. This year 2014 God has already blessed us so awesomely with promotions, restoration of all kinds has come and etc, also where House of Refuge will be rebirth in the land of the promise. This has been and begun our year of restoration and restitution.

Now we truly have seen in this chapter about Ishmael and how to wait patiently on the promises of God but I encourage even the ones that has already accepted Ishmael to complete your task in their lives and value the time with them but release them when God instructs you to because your relationship with God and destiny is much more valuable.

Chapter 17
Though You May Not Want Me, You Need Me

There will come a time in life where your relationship will go through some fiery trials and tribulations where you will want to leave or even separate from someone, for many reasons. Some of the reasons is because of mistreatment. Some maybe because of you thinking you're putting too much pressure and burdens on the other person but whatever the case is, discern the matter, seek God to see if it's the right thing to do and by all means separate if have to. You're being in a person life in the time where they really need you, is more valuable than you think, even if the heat is turn up or they want you to leave them alone. Your being there can save a life and soul. Your being there maybe a time of acceleration, but whatever the situation is, discern the matter and make the wise judgment because a wise person heart judge both time and judgement.

There are many stories like of my pass to where rebelled against me, spoke they didn't want but needed me and when push came to shove they returned back to me and as I said God had sent me to see about them.

Jesus And The Possessed Man
There's a story in the bible where the demons cried out to Christ Jesus and said, LEAVE ME ALONE! Mark 5:1-20.
In 2012 I went through some ups and downs in ministry with the women especially. In the fall of 2012 I had a dream about some women that I pastored, mentored and once was in friendship with. Some rebelled against me tremendously, even some slandered, betrayed and separated from me but I constantly prayed for them inspite of. One day as I was in prayer one of my former daughters in the gospel that was upset with me, drops upon my heart very heavy as I saw her face then I intercede and warred for her the more. After prayer I took it

upon myself to check in on her and told her if I didn't hear back from her that I was going to come by but I didn't received no response back for about a whole two weeks. Then one day I had this dream about some of the women including her. I saw how the women was still gossiping about and mocking me but it was her in particular that was extremely upset with me and then I began to see her and her daughters go into this store to look for some shoes, so in the dream God told me to walk into the store to her and I'm like God did you just hear all of what they said and was plotting against me but I started walking towards going into the store. As I watched her I saw that she was trying to find the right pair of shoes to fit her and her daughters but couldn't. As I was headed over there to her she looked up and saw me and I began to feel like God why are you sending me over there to her when you know she don't want my help and even have said it out of her own mouth. Then God spoke to me and said although she say she don't want my help, she needs your help as well as some of the others. Then HE said continue to go to her she needs

your help and I did and when I got there to her
the kids saw me, hugged and loved me hard
then told me they missed me but she still acted
as though she was really upset with me but I
persisted on showing her my loved and helping
her with getting the best pair of shoes. Then as
I insisted on helping and elaborated on how to
find the right pair of shoes, she broke down in
tears and then hugged me then I woke up and
prayed mercy for her. I asked the Lord do He
just want me to just pray for her or go to her
house??? Then He answered me speedily and
said go to her house now. So I told my
husband and we went over to her house
together. As we was headed to her house we
prayed together and as we reached the house
the kids met us at the door rejoicing as they
opened the door and hugged us but when we
went in she was trying to get off the floor in
agony, pain and tears. So I went over to her to
help her up and to embrace her so embraced
me with a huge hug and said she was sorry for
everything and that she needed me. After I
embraced her we all sat down on the sofa and
she told me everything how everything in her

Though You May Not Want Me, You Need Me

life was crumbling, that she was to prideful but know she needed my help and that she was going to come over to my house but her husband had took the car to work. She said goes on to say about her eyes started to mess up on her and how she was having bad heart palpitations and that her heart was hurting that she was having severe headaches and confused. Me and my husband listened to her as she release alot that day but we embraced her dearly and forgave her prayed for her and deliverance came to her that day as she purge greatly. The day of salvation had come to her but you see God ways are not ours and His love is beyond comprehension, and although some may say leave me alone and I don't want your help but if you look at the heart of the matter they are really saying that I do. I could have went many ways with that but will elaborate here on this, "Although they may say they don't want you but they NEED YOU. Some would have shook that off in looking at a rebel like that and let they be but the heart that the Father has given me is too big for that. I see the value in the people HE sends to me and hold dear the relationships to my heart until God releases me to let go.

In this story Jesus was met by this man that had legions of demons and they cried out begging him to leave them alone but Jesus insisted on going forth in helping this man by silencing the demons that spoke to him through this man, the demons tormenting the man, being violent to others and possessing this man soul and spirit. Jesus saw beyond the words that spoke out of the man mouth that said Leave me alone and saw the value in the life of the man and his relationship with him and Heavenly Father. There was great value in the life of the man and it was saving his soul, renewing his spirit and transforming his life, giving him a testimony that he may save others through the transformation of his salvation. We too need to hear and see beyond the words and see the value in people when they tried to run us away and run from us. We need to see the value in the relationship that we're connected to so that we will be able to save a soul and transform a life through the power of the blood of Christ Jesus.

Jesus And The Relationship With His Disciples

There was a time when Jesus testing the hearts and faith of his disciples after saying some hard sayings, where many turn away from him and didn't him no more. Then Jesus asked them a question, are you going to leave me too? Then Peter with his outspoken self said No Lord, where would we go? You have the words to eternal life. WOW! These were powerful words Peter spoken. I feel that within my being every time I read that. Lord You have the words to eternal life! I'm not going nowhere. Then Jesus in returned the words and said I chose you. John 6:67-70.

This is truly a relationship. There was much value in both parties in this relationship. The Love for the sons and the sons love for his Father. Such Authenticity! When we all comes to grips within ourselves we will see how every God sent person that has been sent into our life is valuable to our destiny. Take the time to seek to God asking him what part they come to help fulfill.

Ruth And Naomi Relationship
Let's look at another story that said a similar saying the story of Ruth and Naomi.

I love the relationship between Ruth and Naomi, it's rare to find a people that will do and spoke what Ruth said. Ruth 1:6-18. In the story of Ruth and Naomi we see how Naomi insisted that Ruth turn back to her home town although Naomi spoke that with her lips, Ruth knew that Naomi needed her on the journey. I believe Ruth didn't just the say what she said because of the deserted journey that Naomi had to take nor her that she didn't want to see her alone but she saw the worth her own destiny lies with her mother-in-law Naomi. There was much value in serving Naomi staying at her side and at feet. I feel safe to say that through all the years Ruth walked with Naomi watching her strengths in building her house, being loyal and faithful to her God and saw a difference in the life that Naomi had inspite all her weaknesses. Although Ruth knew Naomi wasn't financial stable but she saw something way more worth more precious in her than money. She saw virtue, she saw integrity. She saw and her wisdom built her house. She saw strength in still standing and staying loyal to the God that she served. In Ruth seeing all of that and more she wanting and know she needed that. Naomi insisted on telling Ruth to go back but Ruth insisted on holding onto her and not turning back. I say to all my readers if you ever find that Ruth hang on to her and if you ever find that Naomi hang on to her and serve her well for great is your reward.

On the other hand we that Orpah the other daughter turned back. Could this have been a test all the while to see who would be truly loyal? There will come a time as I said earlier that relationship will go through testing of trials and tribulations and this test comes to test the hearts, faith and loyalty to still if you really going to stand the test. Even if I told you to leave would you see beyond my words, discern the times, seasons, situation and the matters of my heart. Would you really leave me in a place of despair and abandonment? Would you really leave me in a deserted and desolate place? My husband and I, once had a former member tell us that they will never leave us and know that we needed his help but in the opposite his actions and the attitude of his heart didn't reflect his words that he spoke. So in these type of situations you will have to discern these times when your leaders and people speak with their lip turn back. You will have to leave them alone and or ask, are you going to leave me as well?

Elijah And Elisha Relationship
There's another story that resembles Ruth and Naomi that is Elijah and Elisha. 2 King 2:1-18.

This too is another story of rare relationship. Elisha insisted on going on with his father in the gospel Elijah after Elijah told him to turn back and go on your way now but Elisha said no sir I will never leave your side and as long as the Lord lives and your soul lives I will not leave you. Ruth and Elisha both saw the value in their leaders and knew their own destiny was locked up inside of them and knew there serving wasn't going to be in vain. When it was time for Elijah to be taken away from Elisha he asked him what shall I give you before I am taken away from you and Elisha asked for double portion of his anointing and Elijah said its a difficult thing you ask me but nevertheless if you see taking away from you it will be so and it was so. You being in a God sent relationship its' vital that you stay connected to it because it's much value in it and even though there will be some bumps and bruises it still will be worth it all in hanging in there. You Elisha worshipped the Lord in spirit and in truth as he did in his heart and service to his leader Elijah so therefore God had to give him what he desired. And Jesus said in John there's nothing that the Lord won't do for a true worshipper. A true worshipper will softens the Lord heart and he will move expediently for him.

Chapter 18
Respect & Honor

Where there is No value, there is no respect. In any relationship that you're developing there needs to be a level of respect for one another. Even if there are disagreements there should be a level of respect that you have for one another, being that you're in a more personal relationship with them. I've learned over the years, where you're not welcome, respected, or honored is usually because of unbelief and familiarity. It will be an extremely hard ground trying to plow up, operate and flow freely, when this is the case. You can be one of the most powerful people with much to give but if there is unbelief, no honor and respect, you will not be able to flow as you should. Jesus Himself couldn't do many miracles in His own hometown because of this.

I can remember in my own hometown it was a battle flowing there as I longed too but because of disbelief, no respect and honor, I couldn't flourish as much. God allowed me to save and impart some but it wasn't impactful as other towns where other was hungry for what God has put within me to where I was able to flow freely and demonstrate the powers of God through signs, miracles and wonders.

Being in a place among people that don't honor you with hearts, lips and action it's very difficult to operate. Continuing in a place that has no respect you will cause you to compromise your character and standards because you will instead struggle in trying to prove yourself to people that are unchanging to whom they see you as and what you have within that you know for yourself can save their lives and change their life for the good.

Honoring Me with Lips
I can recall numerous of times when I got among people that said they respect and honor but their heart was far from me. Coming in the mist of these people that honor you with their lips you will sense and feel a resistance in

them and it will began to hinder you flow. Holy Spirit within you will quicken you and reveal to you the heart of these people that only speak with their lips. There will be times Holy Spirit will restrain you from giving out too much. They're other times Holy Spirit will cause you to give them more time but through parables and dark speech and cause you bear with them a little while longer so that they will be held accountable to what they have heard. There will be other times Holy Spirit will cause you to prophesy against them and restrain you from giving them anything.

These people will come to you with enticing words to try seem as if their truly for you but their truly spies, wolves in sheep clothing and thieves. The bible says and Jesus didn't come out because He knew them. He knew that they had unchanging ways and itching ears. I've been around people that said such flatteries but when push can to shove to truly see if they honored me as their lips spoken, they failed. When these times of testing come where they would have to prove their honor to me in public they instead denied me, abandoned me, disrespected me and ensnared me with the pearls that I had given to them. There were other times where got what I pour and imparted within them and gave another man credit for it. We must be very in casting pearls and giving bread to those that truly don't honor and respect us.

Prophetic Wisdom:
Looking over the years of my Christian life, God revealed to me that I'm eight years behind time. He revealed certain and specific locations, places, situations, years and etc, concerning these eight years behind time. So you do the math. I suppose to be wayyy further than I am now. I've realized through the course of time that I've let satan steal time from me by wasting it. I've wasted time in my Christian life in expired places such as churches, jobs, cities, and homes. I've wasted time and pearls on people and places that no longer respect, value, or appreciate me. I wasted time on people throughout the years because of misidentifying, immaturity and compromise;

such as befriending and being too transparent to my flock, trainees and mentorees, befriending my enemies, belittling and taking points from myself by showing false humility in the mist of senior leaders, submitting to popularity instead of fruits, allowing myself to call, be mentored and trained by wrong mentors and spiritual parents, staying in expired relationships, being presumptuous, allowing rejection and fear get in my heart that ran me to the cave,.I cast away my confidence, had low self-esteem, feared man, tried to prove to people that don't honor nor see the value in me and etc. Learn from my testimony and mistakes. Don't spend your life in a place asking God to redeem time because of wasted time. Count up the cost of time and make sure you sow your time wisely. You see God has a timetable/timeline for you to follow that's written in the book of life but satan has a timeline strategically for you as well to abort and distract you from the timeline of God. As I stated about my misfortunes of wasted time, things like this will take you off God timetable. So repent of getting out the will of God, ask

God to reveal to you how many years you behind time, know your worth and get yourself back in the will and timetable of God so you won't always ask God to redeem time for you. #Manage your time wisely, fight for your life and freedom!!!#

<u>Secret Lovers</u>

I can remember times when others would come talk to me behind closed doors when others wouldn't see them to get imparted into but when they would get around me in public they would act as if they don't know me. I would begin to see this over and over again when certain people would come and be in desperate times because of them not getting fed from their own leaders or escaped they then come to me but then deny me or act as if they don't know me in public. I would be hurt by it but because I loved them and saw a need I supplied spiritual and natural food for them. Until one day I was outside in my back yard communing with the Lord, He spoke to me and said to be careful of Secret Lovers, I then began to ask questions of what He meant and

He said to me watch this. Right after He said watch this, a neighbor's dog came through my gate to me purring for food from me as they would normally do when their hungry if their not getting from their own owners. So the dog purred and purred for food for about a minute or so as I of course felt sorry for him because I didn't have nothing at the time for him, so when he realize I didn't have anything he barked at me and left. So I went inside the house and then the rest of the dogs came, about all 15 of them, hungry as usual but this time I didn't feed them. Some barked, the other ones wagged their tail and held their heads down, the medium sized one scoffed at my direction looking back. Then I was instructed to walk outside my gate to see the owners coming home and when I went passed their house the owner stopped and wanted to chit chat with me, and as we were conversing all her dogs came beside her and barked at me as if they didn't know me and the older one wagged their tails and held their heads down and sat down looked at and turn their heads down. The other owner dogs bark at me when the his owner came home and looked back at me and then dropped his head. Now after this I walked back down the road towards my house and asked God what He was trying to show me although I had an idea about Stray dogs as He revealed a similar situation before to me with a stray dog but He need revealed that it was similar to the stray dogs but these kinds were called Secret Lovers and He then expound about Nicodemus coming to Jesus. These kinds normally give you honor and respect behind closed doors, when no one watching or around but will turn on me at any given moment and that I must be careful of them. Then later on that day, it was another woman of God came to my house and it was almost dark. She longed for spiritual food. She begin to apologize to me for not giving honor. She told me she was forced by and strictly forbade by her leaders to not have anything to do with me nor go to my gatherings where I held a company of prophets and prophetic people being equipped and perfected, growing rapidly in the prophetic, prophesying and teaching freely. She told me how she was so hurt by how the leaders and church conspired and slandered me and my husband ministry at this time and that she felt bad but couldn't be seen with me in public and was told to act as if I don't know her. I felt so bad for the woman of God although I knew that this was going on behind close doors about our ministry but I still felt bad for her, then told her I loved her, encouraged her in the Lord but I couldn't no longer see her like this by giving her any of my pearls because it wasn't fair to me nor her, she scoffed and held her head down as the older dogs that I had seen earlier that day.

After this day of this woman of God coming to my house by herself as the first dog done then there was some others that did, some called and message as well but as was the first woman and dog, I done the same to them. However with some of the others, their response to me was more rude, vindictive and the such as were some of the medium dogs, small dogs and a couple of the older and bigger dogs. I thank for warning me, preparing me and instructing me on what to do in these times.

To everything there is a purpose, timing, season and harvest, therefore I had to know the time to feed and let them glean but also the time to let go and cut it off. About a week later after cutting off the supply of these individuals, God told me that He was going to send us some people that weren't from the region. He showed some of them vividly, plainly and called them by name to me in my prayer time and upon my dreams and visions. Then He instructed where exactly the location where they would be to save them and present Him to them and it was so. In places such as the library, grocery stores and shopping centers and walking. Obeying the instructions of the Lord is imperative because He's always looking to reconciled to someone and get into relationship with them. He always wants us to be respected and freely to flow. Although we couldn't do many great works there in my hometown we did impacted some that was reserved just for us.

Chapter 19
<u>Wisdom in Transparency</u>

In your time of developing and cultivating relationships it's a need to gain wisdom in being transparent, because giving too much and being too open can cost you. Don't become your own demise because you were blabber mouth. It's vital in using wisdom in transparency. I've seen many while evangelizing go trying to be relatable to others instead of letting the spirit of the Lord lead them and draw others to himself. Instead they go and become to transparent and open telling all their busy to the swine that evidently bites them in the butt and regretting later of what they release. Too much information expose all at once can bring a reproach and harm to you. Please believe me, I am a witness to it. I was once a person and still yet growing not to e to open with everyone I meet even if I discern that they are God sent and are covenant people. You want to always be led by Holy Spirit that will draw, lead you and teach what you must say, because ministering and moving in our own strengths, gifts and abilities can bring us harm. There are boundaries in ministering and giving to anyone. My husband and I working as team is so much vital to my ministry because it's teaches me to put and keep a guard at my mouth, knowing I'm such a giver and a prophet that can go all day if you let me. My husband always says the right person at the wrong time is still the wrong person so therefore too many words at the wrong time can be catastrophe. The right words at the wrong time can bring much harm. I've seen this in the ministry of others and through my own experiencing. As grandmother and mother used to tell us when we was small it needs to apply today and that is Choose yours carefully and you need to learn shut up sometimes.

So many relationships have been destroyed because that talked too much. Just telling all their business. Take the time to get to know someone before you give too much and even in getting to know a person and finding out they have been proven to be trustworthy you still want to use wisdom in exposing too much at one time. The bible tells us to not put all our trust in man. It is unwise to do so. This is not to say everyone will treat you badly, misuse or abused because of previous mishaps in the past but it just to keep the spice and excitement in the relationship.

<u>Boundaries</u>
Women are especially victims to this. We will tell it all if you let us because we are talkers. We love to vent. We love counsel. We love to help others and if we see a mends a share a testimony to help someone else get healed and deliverance we will release.

We must become masters of keeping a watch at our mouths. Setting boundaries is imperative in our openness. I use this prayer before ministering, counsel and evangelizing.

You will have to begin to quote Isaiah that speaks of; Lord give me the tongue of the learned to be able to speak a word in season to the hearers that is full of grace and seasoned with salt so that it would bring deliverance and healing to them.

Lord give me a mouth and wisdom where the enemy would not be able to gainsay me.

Hill Of Difficulty
On this journey you will meet people that are detrimental to your walk and people that only come to detour and distract you. On your journey walking with the Lord, you will come to a place called the Hill of Difficulty. As you walk this journey, you will meet people that seem as if they're on the same journey with you, but then you realize that they come with Vain Glory as thieves and robbers known as hypocrisy and formalise. Instead of them taking the path of righteousness that was given to and set before them, they began to make their own paths that evidently lead to danger and destruction.

So I come to you to you my Christian brothers and sisters to say, stay on the straight and narrow path that leads to abundant living and eternal life. Though there will be times in life on your journey where you will reach the hills of difficulties, but I encourage you to push inspite of and press the battle to the gate and when the enticing and deceiving way that leads to destruction comes to try to detour and distract you will know to resist it and surly it will flee from you.

Casting Pearls To The Swine
Be careful where and who you cast your pearls too. Make sure you are sowing your pearls on the right ground to bring forth much more pearls. When you cast your pearls to the wise you will see the good harvest on your sowing, because the one to whom you have sown into will become doers of what you have sown into them and then they will multiply what has been given and return the honor to you which you have sown into them. Sowing into the wrong people will only bring false burdens upon you. So make sure you are not wasting pearls on swine. These swines are people that just are hearers, rebels, treason's, pliables and people

Wisdom in Transparency

that don't really have your heart. So be wise and be careful.

Chapter 20
Timing

The Right Person At The Wrong Time
There are times where people will come into our lives at the wrong time and season. My husband has this saying that goes as this; The right person at the wrong time is still the wrong person.

I've met many people that I know that God said to be in a relationship with but because of the timing it wasn't the right time to connect with them. If you rush relationships to connect before timing, you can mess things up.

My testimony of this is me and my husband relationship. There was a time going into high school, when we tried to hook up but it didn't work out. We would come together more so trying to protect our love ones and just talk as friends. Then there were another time when I was in College Technical School and he was in

Timing

Georgia Southern University. We saw each other at this annual player's ball that they had on campus, so we then walked the whole block together to where he wanted to get with me but at this time I wasn't interested. Athough he wanted to and my cousins wanted me to get with him, it wasn't time or what we both really wanted nor was ready for at the time. Then 2005 God showed me in a dream about my husband struggles, needing help and his salvation. Then one day I saw him in his church as I visited as they had a revival at their church to where me and a friend of mines went. God used me and my friend there ministering. I saw him and we spoke briefly afterwards about his gospel rap, staying the straight and narrow and how I was moved by his compassion and heart towards the Lord, but that still wasn't the time. So about a month or two passed in 2006, I had to minister through song at his church but he wasn't there that time but his mom was. I had never met her before although knowing him and his brother. After service the night of me ministering in song, his mom followed me outside to ask me

Timing

for my address, information and ask me to sing again. In the mist of her asking me for information, telling me how well I done and beautiful I sounded, God gave me a prophetic word for her and about one of her sons. As she was blessing the Lord and crying to what the Lord was saying through me, my cousin which was the Pastor sister, came outside to where we were as I was still prophesying to his mom. After I was done and his mom was still overwhelmed by what God said being in tears, my cousin said to me, do you know who mother you're talking too? I said to her, No I don't. She then called his sister name which I never heard of nor met before. Then she said his brother name and my husband name and I was like yes wow I didn't know. So a little after this when his mom at calm down, she gave me my husband number to call him and help encourage him in the Lord and she said she was going to give him my number as well. Now to remind you it was only to help encourage him in the Lord but God had other plans two months after that to where me and my husband

Timing

started conversing as friends, brother and sister in Christ to being a powerful union now.

You see God timing is far better than our, and although it maybe the wrong timing it still the right person so I encourage you to be patient in your waiting season. The saying is true, the delay is not the denial. For in your waiting season God is still around and conduct herself a way because I was not to disrespect the one that sat on the bench. The lesbian it felt like she knew me but didn't know where but now she know and she said, we was in the same family and was kindred in spirit and that's how she recognize me and then she asked me, are you a preacher a pastor and I said yes and she rejoice in laughter and said I knew it and now I know. She put her head down in sadness about her transgression as a prodigal daughter and lesbian state. So she stop as I now encouraged both of them and the demon possessed girl opened up about her tortured soul and how she was possessed by many that she couldn't control these many demons that lived in her and she called all of them out by

Timing

name to me. I had to be very discreet in my approach in the cell because the guards was looking and my time had not yet come as I heard the spirit of the Lord told me. So the gentlemen of the holy spirit showed me how to handle this situation in bringing deliverance to these two young ladies. My angels accompanied me in the cell alone with the two as I prayed and charged the atmosphere to be conductive to the glory of God to bring an instantaneous change. So as I ministered to the demon possess woman with love of Jesus. I laid hands on her shoulders first then her head, then her back as I'm praying for her rebuking satan off her life but when I was to grab her hands that's when she brought down in tears and screeching sound and buckled her knees down on the floor but then I lifted her up as she was surrendering her life to Jesus and I was instructed to give her a big hug to where she broke down some more but I held her tighter and told her Jesus loves her but don't return to the old ways and told her how much Jesus has need of her and her kids needed there mom and how He was going to move on

Timing

her behalf but she must not return to the old ways. About 5 minutes after this as the lesbian watched and prayed with head down, the guards came to get the once demon possess woman that the Lord had just delivered. When the guard arrived to get her, she asked the guard for a pen for my number and give me her name, she thanked me with tears in her eyes, hugged me once more and said thank God for the preacher and that she was going to go to the services Sunday and she did tell me that she had already sat up counseling sessions with the pastors that was coming that Sunday. Thinking about this bring joy to my heart of that day of them two souls.

After she us then there was just me and the lesbian left alone in the holding cell going to the same city to see the judge with the same probation officer. Our journey together was longer and I saw how God healed wounds of this young woman taking a different approach with her. He also used her as a spokesperson for me at a time. This young had lost her fight and zeal for the Lord and needed someone to truly bring healing to the deep seated issues that was in her life. She had been prostituted by the church. She had been raped by pastors and abandoned by parents. She knew what she was doing was wrong to where she admitting in guilt, shamed and true sorrow. She thanked God for me in my counsel and consolation to her. She praised and worship the Lord. I did prayed for her and rebuked satan off her life and then spoke the word of the Lord to her. God used me mightily through words of knowledge and words of wisdom with this young woman. This young was very intelligent and had her way with words and there was times I had to chastise her for her anger in love. She had deep roots of bitterness, anger, rejection, deep hurts and resentment in her. This gifted young woman was indeed delivered and welcome back into the arms of the Heavenly Father but my heart is very much with her especially for her maintaining her deliverance. The demon possessed woman was a woman that never knew Jesus and the lesbian was a prodigal daughter that the Father was drawing back unto His bosom. I see these two women as a shadow type of the Mary Magdalene and the man that Jesus said take up your mat and walk and the situation was similar.

My Timing Had Not Yet Come

In many times with these young women the Lord instructed me to be very discreet with the approach of ministry to them, because my time had not yet come. Many in the jail pulled on me, put demand on the anointing on me but I had to be discreet with some because my time had not yet come as I heard the voice of the Lord said. I was not to cause a big scene and have many gravitate to me as making a big scene, even when some tried that begged more me at times to minister to them, but the Lord would tell me to shut up in my room in a consecrated time of just me and him and I did just that even when they called me and wanted me to come out to help, heal and minister to them.

You see God timing is not our timing at all, and as you can see that the Lord kept telling me

Timing

that my timing had not yet came yet. You see if I was too have revealed and exposed myself before time, I would probably had stayed in there longer because of disobedience and revealing myself on a greater capacity before time. To everything there is a time and a season. A time to speak and time to be silent. A time to reveal and a time being hidden. A time to make known and a time to remain unknown. A time for exposure and a time for disclosure. A time to reveal the glory of God and time to conceal the glory of God. To everything there is a time, purpose and season. Don't ever go before-time because it will cost you. Being presumptuous too bold and forward can bring you much harm, danger and death before-time. Even Jesus Himself said this many of times as too I was reminded by when I heard the voice of the Lord spoke it to me. Jesus knew his time of fulfillment and knew when others was trying to push Him out there before-time to as he made this known. Even in discontinuation of demonstrations of his powers he was discreet in doing some of them. Wisdom teaches how to pursue such situations that needs immediate attention and so He follow and let wisdom teaches and leads him how to walk in wisdom in supplying the needs of the people. Truly he was moved with compassion for the people. Truly He cares for you and value the relationship that he has with you. What a Love that concerns about us even when we don't deserve it.

It's imperative to connect at the right time with the right people, saying the right things and speaking a word in due season that will truly impact someone life bringing an instantaneous change and recovery to them. Ironing some kinks out of you as well as him. This is truly an encouragement to the singles that awaits marriage.

Also to the children of God that's in transition in ministry under a oppressive leadership or at home waiting but fellow-shipping with many other churches seeking God for the right Godly leader. You may have fellowship with and was introduced to the right leader but the time is not yet come to fulfillment to where God can truly put you together, because He's still working on you and your soon to be leader heart for the you all awaited connection. I can also can recall this time as well with my and I father in the gospel and how he came year before God said he was for us to render our leadership under his governance. There was a transition before the fulfillment. God had to close a door, uproot, heal and mend somethings and bring clarity before it was concrete in the time of fulfillment under his oversight and leadership.

Training For Reigning
There were also times when my husband and I was prophesied numerous times in our previous ministry about launching out in planting, building and starting our own ministry but the time had not come to where God what that to go forth yet. We heard this in every year our our marriage in the ministry to where we served as faithful servants and servant leaders there. Until that time where God said now is the time for the son of God to be glorified through the new work that I have called y'all to do with a new leader as y'all overseer.

Timing

You see king David was ordained and set apart as a new king instead of king Saul but he still had to wait although he was already called. He had to wait more years to truly reign as king in the stead of king Saul. As were king David, my husband and I, so will you have to go through a training period before you truly reign in your own domain as king and ruler.

I can remember when I was incarcerated to where God used me mightily through signs, wonders and miracles. There was a time while I was incarcerated in my holding cell awaiting the appearance of the judge to where I had been in fasting for 15 days and was on fast with no food for three days and behold I was presented with situation that needed immediate attention to where I had to used much wisdom to how to pursue the matter at hand. You see there was a young woman that was possess with many demons and another woman that was now a lesbian but yet a prodigal daughter that was trying to return back to God. We all was in the holding cell awaiting the judge or some had just seen the judge awaiting to go

Timing

back to their individual cell. It was at a time where me and like 10 other women was in one holding cell to where I first recognized the lesbian and the demon possess girl. So when the time came where it was just me and the two of them left in the holding cell, their the demon possessed girl talked with me because she said she identified me along with the lesbians. They said they had identified me without me opening my mouth and the lesbians girl said she was restrained by force not to say somethings

Chapter 21
Corrective Criticism

Every relationship will go through a time where corrective criticism will be given, but don't get bent out of shape by it. The proverbs says iron sharpens iron and a friend sharpens the countenance of his or her friend.

I was once in this relationship when it was put to the test where only one of my friends would only want to do the correcting but didn't want to be corrected. This is not how it goes. You see when there are two irons rubbing up against one another, one just don't do the sharpen or ironing while the other one don't get sharpens but both gets sharpen and although it may not feel good at the time of the sharpening it is good for you to be sharpen. So in saying that, there will be times where you will see things about one another character, attitude and actions that's needs to be corrected and sharpened you then will have to take the

Corrective Criticism

necessary actions to sharpen and iron out your friend attitude.

You see when in the time of the testing of the relationship and the testing of the person character in the relationship comes, it will show if you're truly mature enough in how you receive correction and or corrective criticism. It will show if you will take it too personally by getting out of character by taking offense at what was said by acting out unseemly in retaliation to the one that's giving the correction. Your response will stick out like a sore thumb, so be careful how you respond to it.

In every relationship there will be corrective criticism but woe to the ones that giving it out. Take courage in this times I would say, because although your intentional and wordiness is demonstrated and illustrated in love it will not be perceived as it was done out of love.

Corrective Criticism

I say this again any relationship that you get into will go through a time of sharpening, testing and pruning where there will be corrective criticism that must go forth to help the other whether they receive it at the opportune time or not, however it must be done.

Chapter 22
Pitfalls in Relationships

No Boundaries
A relationship that has no standards or boundaries is awaiting a fall. Every relationship should know its purpose. Every person should know their position and assignment in the relationship. This kind of relationship will no its boundaries as to far too go. This don't box the relationship in but its cause the relationship to be built on the right foundation, be develop right and cultivated healthy where it will increase in growth and flow smoothly. Accurately defining the relationship is wisdom that one must gain as an example that Jesus set up for us. This will cause a checks and balance in the relationship. Although one will know how to be sensitive to the timing to know how administer each function as will meet the need of the situation in the relationship, however, its very vital to know its purpose and

who Jesus say the person was in their life as its gradually develops. Purpose is Everything is a need to know and vital to going into any relationship. It is unwise to just flow with what is flowing without knowing the purpose of the relationship or your position in a person life. Jesus knew the purpose of being relationship with the 12 disciples and He knew who He was to them and they knew He was to them as well their position. In knowing this it show boundaries and set standards. He administer Himself to them as will being brother, teacher, master, friend, prophet, Son of God, son of Man, burden bearer, etc as the relationship gradually develops. This as well is a preventive measure of any roadblocks, misunderstandings and confusion. Setting boundaries and having standards is a needed in any relationship.

Selfishness (GIVE Me Mentality)
Selfishness is the number one destroyer of relationships. Selfishness and self-centeredness of all kinds steals away from the fullness of the relationship. Any time you come into a relationship with this mentality its storing

up for itself a great fall. I remember being in a relationship where an individual only thought of their own selves. Attention, Affection, Appreciation, evolves around them and their world. They based a relationship off of materialistic things and monetary gain, you giving them money and buying them things. They saw value in these materialistic things whether seeing it in the time invested, wisdom, love, being a listening ear, patience, long-sufferings, saving their marriages, helping them with their kids, your wisdom and teachings how to get wealth, being the vessel that introduced and reconciled them back to Jesus, you protecting them having their backs from persecutions of slander, accusations and the sorts. You have to be careful with these types of people, because they have ill motives, wicked agendas, evil intentions, and when they give to you especially money or materialistic things its not giving out of generosity or cheerfulness but its giving to say I've done this for you so I want this in return when I want it. Their giving is done because they want others to know what they done for you, Their giving is done to keep you in bondage to them out of control and manipulation. So please be careful of selfish self-centered that's ready to strike you at any time because they can't get their way or get what they want because they still haven't put away a childish mindset and ways. Their still more growing up for them to do. They want you to babysit them all the time and on the defense and offense and ready to strike you at even time if it don't caters to them or not centered around them. They will drain you and wear you out if you let them. So please again to tread carefully with them and if God ordained the relationship, make sure you seek God instructions and wisdom on going about helping the individual restoring them to good health.

No Space
Doing anything too much can become to your demise. Being around or talking to a person too much can be a pitfall because you will gradually lose respect for one another by becoming familiar with one another by becoming familiar and comfortable with a

person you will soon lose respect in their eyes and with their actions. Once you lost respect for someone or respect for them its hard to get it back, because you will try to raise the standards bar again or separate for a time and when this happens it will release confusion to an individual even in your communicating this to them. Now there are those that are more mature to be able to handle a time as such but even if it a more seasoned person getting to clingy can become the destroyer of the relationship. The awkwardness comes because of paranoid, imagery and magnification of the person that has become to comfortable with you.

Overly-Protective

Because of this strong soul tie yes ungodly soul tie has developed it becomes crippling to a person where they has now made you their God and Savior and now you can't go a day without them, because of them desiring your presence. This trap is reckless to the relationship, and it starts off with you helping someone that needs mending of a broken-heart. They desire to want you to their house or on the phone with them constantly catering to their needs and desires. Giving too much time and not enough space to meditate do observation and let God with them and the situation. So how that you have being proven to there for them they become more opened, personal, secure and comfortable because you're always there to be their rescuer.

I remember all too well where this happened in my life. I became overly-protective to some formers daughters and mentors that I flocked, but it was two particular that became so common, comfortable and relax with bailing them out and being there for them, that when it was time for me to help others they became upset and jealous as it I was leaving or have left them.

Jealousy
Many noticed this as I done as well. One verbally spoken that they didn't like individual and me giving one too much time while the other acting out when I showed others

attention immaturity yes ungodly Eh. They both became jealous of one another and jealous of me ministering to others, until people said I'm distancing myself from you until I separate myself from her. Both of these individuals constantly done this even to the point that one shipwreck the ministry with seduction.

When I realized the severity of these spirits in these individual it had already invaded my life and ministry. When it was time to separate for a time they didn't want it and didn't know how to handle the situation with me being separated for a whole day or two, left alone a week. These two relationship constantly tried to sabotage and destroy my ministry and life through many mends as betrayal, wanting to physical attack me and any mends necessary.

My advice to babes and mature people alike to avoid familiarity by any means necessary. When you see it take action to distance yourself so God can show you, you show them and be the Lord and Savior in their lives.

Pitfalls in Relationships

I remember one day in ministry with one of my former students in Christ where we traveled to Carolina and in getting to our destination to where she recommend to me to this elderly woman that woman that had ask for me to come counsel, that wanted to be baptized, impart the gift of holy spirit and of fire and heal her. So when we arrived there I sat down to talk to the women of God then she began to say she had something to give me from the Lord and she told me about this young lady that I was ministering to was very unhealthy to my ministry and life at the time and that I needed to separate myself and that God needed me in other areas. I immediately knew who she spoke of but it was so hard to do, even though this lady had no knowledge of me and her two daughters in Christ relationship other that what the Lord revealed to her. She told me I was needed in other places, cities and nations and that this spirit was coming to sabotage, delay and hinder destiny. After I listened to her words of wisdom, she now wanted to be baptized and healed. Of course you know she gave food to us before we left.

Backbiting

As hard as it was I followed the instructions of the elderly woman because I knew her words was not her own. In taking steps in severing the ties and separating wasn't easy at all for a time. In communicating this with wisdom to my former daughter in the Lord she didn't know how to handle it, so she began to lash out on me, slandering me badly and betrayed me but I knew what it was and prayed for her and the mercy of the Lord to heal her in this transitioning time. In doing this separation and getting my own deliverance, God sent more women to me to minister too and also sent me to minister into different churches.

Unrealistic Expectations

Understanding God's Love and the language it carries in others lives is a life long process of exploring, but one must begin to explore the nature and language of it to be able to discern the state the person craves. Even though that person will never get this type of Love in return as they long for in human kind, but they must not neglect to show God love to others. It took sometime for me to understand this because I put demands on others and long for it in human effort, but they came up short in my life every time, because of my unrealistic expectations.

Getting into any relationship with unrealistic expectation will destroy the relationship before it begins. People that expect are people that are perfectionist, critical, judgemental and are fearful. These people unusually never really sees the good of are the attempt of others trying or accomplishing anything, so they demand more becoming overbearing and domineering making it harder to fulfill a task or succeed a assignment. I've been in relationship where I was a predator and prey of this. Unrealistic relationship often occurs in marriages where you will see a spouse especially the wife demands more from her husband, not realizing his trying, his improvements and his accomplishments. We as wives have tendency to want more instead of being appreciative of what have been accomplished and improved right before our very eyes. Also another thing is when coming out of a previous relationship of many let downs and downfalls, the other person will carry that same hurt into their current relationship expecting things from the new person things that they are not able to fulfill. Please be very careful of this because it will destroy your relationships abruptly, causing you to miss out on some good relationships.

Too Much Openness

As I've stated before in previous chapters, too much openness can be the relationship demise. Be careful of giving too much of your weaknesses to others especially all act once and to unstable people. Exercise discipline, watch over and put a guard on your mouth when you feel you're about to open up too much to others. I pray you gain wisdom in transparency, and that God will give you a mouth and wisdom and to able to have the tongue of the learned so that your good want be spoken evil of, that you want cast pearls before the swine nor the stray dogs where your enemy can't find room to ensnare you..

No/Lack Of Communication

No or the lack communication is another destroyer of relationships. Keeping the lines of communication open will prevent any misunderstandings, confusion and or seeds of discord. Its imperative to communicate. Communication is Key in any relationship. Even during times of misunderstandings to where you are trying to resolve issues that have occurred. Every relationship will have its challenging times no matter what, to see if it can withstand the storms that beat upon that relationship, but no matter what communicating is key to resolving the issues and standing the test that beat upon. Any time there is no communication you are storing up for yourself a disaster in the relationship. Any time there is lack of communication it is advantage of your adversary the devil which is the accuser of the brethren to come plant seeds of discord in the hearts and ears of others trying to confuse a matter to divide. So remember where there is lack clear up the misunderstandings to the best of your ability as much as possible especially if you know the relationship will divine and God putting it together. Don't give room for the enemy the devil to divide to conquer the relationship.

Bitterness
Coming into any relationship bound by the root of bitterness from your previous and past relationships will also destroy the relationship if you don't forgive, let go and let God heal you of your wounds and deeps hurts and uproot fears and rejection. Bitterness clouds your judgement, distort your perception, then dull and deafens your ability to hear. Even being in your current where you may get hurt that individual you will truly have to forgive them, holding no records of wrongdoings, harboring no grudges or resentment in your heart because it will sabotage and destroy the relationship.

Familiarity
One thing I've learned from being in different relationships is that familiarity is not your friend at all. Familiarity is a sabortager that destroys relationship every time. Becoming too familiar

with a person will taint your image of them where you will eventually lose respect for a person and see no value in them and the relationship no more, because of weaknesses you see of them. The relationship will become self-centered around everything that caters to their emotions and everything of them. They will demand your listening ears with only tickle me Elmo messages, then when you give corrective criticism or correction they will perceived now you are their enemy attacking them too and perhaps lashing out at them. Once there was a time where one of my former daughter in Christ began to get too familiar with me until she no longer in a sense, see me as her leader but just her friend. She began to talk to me such as just a friend, demand me as just a friend, longed for just friendship, couldn't no longer receive correction or corrective criticism, treated me as just a friend, slander me as just her friend and the sort. I lost my place as her leader in her eyes, until her world in our relationship has now evolved and became just friendship. Becoming to common or showing your weaknesses to unstable people can

Pitfalls in Relationships

become your demise so you want to be very careful of who you show your nakedness too especially before time. Never get comfortable, relax and too familiar with revealing your weaknesses to people especially unstable people, because you will get bit by them every time. Choose your words and your time very carefully. If not they will lose all respect for you and the value in the relationship.

Chapter 23
Abuse

These are some things to be careful of, to avoid and need to know in relationship.

Abuse
There are different kinds of abuse in relationships. Physical abuse, Sexual abuse, mental abuse, verbal abuse, and emotional abuse but in my opinion emotional abuse is one of the worst kinds of abuse there is. I've been in every kind of abuse in my life and had to get heal from them and still a work in process but its nothing like emotional abuse. Emotional abuse can last for years, harming, stealing away from, sabotaging and destroying your other relationships. I've been sexually and physically abuse and recover from it but when it came to emotional abuse it took months and years to recover from. Emotional abuse could even send you to hell because unforgiveness, rejection, fears, bitterness where it could lead

Abuse

to all the others. Again being a victims of emotional abuse can lead to you do the very thing you was once the victim of.

The bible speaks of a woman that had the issue of blood for 12 years. The bible also mention Tamar which was King David daughter that was raped physically by her own brother but the thing that recked her life the most was emotional abuse where he abandon, neglected and rejected her after he had took away her innocence. Emotional abuse happens in all types of relationships such as parents and kids, spouses and in-laws, husband and wife, pastors and sheep, church members among church members, friend and friends, employer and employee, singles and married couples and etc.

Emotional Abuse

Emotional abuse leads to emotional damaging that leads leads to emotional unstable that leads to emotional death that leads to committing suicide. Emotional abuse destroys a person. It first comes as a thief that rob you

Abuse

of your confidence, self esteem and identity. It also comes as a killer that kills your joyful and perseverance spirit that evidently destroys you and your fight to destiny.

As I talked about in the previous chapters about my life as a child being bullied to where I became a bully. In any relationship there needs to not be a place where you hr words in arguments, neglected, rejected and abandoned someone so to the point where you have cause yourself and yourself to lose yourself in the matter to where the relationship will now has taking a turn of being extremely unhealthy. Being abused by your companion so much will cause undue stress upon a person to where it will affect their physical body. Cancer comes from being emotional abuse and damage. Heart attack, ulcer, unbalanced hormones and strokes comes from emotional damage. Being in any relationship that begin to affect to like that I advice you to separate because it will leads to much danger to them and yourself.

Abuse

Emotional abuse has affected all ages. This why you see children going into schools a killing people. This is why children evidently kill parents. This why there are so many suicides among kids especially, because they are emotional damage.

I know this place all so well, because I too has became a victim of iave hit below the belt with yout. I can also recall nervous breakdowns, many contemplating and a attempt of suicide but my Savior and Hero came to see about me in a desperate and critical situation. One of the worst thing to do when you're in a unstable place like this is to isolate yourself from others being alone but it is the time cry out to the Lord for help and find some strong believers to strengthen you because its never wise to be alone at a time like this. Satan will love to cause you to withdraw from strong believers to cause you to harm yourself planting seeds of destruction in your heart as to no one love you and its better off to leave this world but I come to say the devil is a liar and the author thereof. There's always more for you than against no matter what. God is concern about the state of His bride which is his people and He wants to come to give you a hope, future and an expectant end.

Unbelievers and Believers alike has face a giants enemy like this but I come to say you will overcome this place. You will defeat this enemy. You are more than a conqueror. My passion is for the underdogs and the outcast because I too used to be one and know how it feels to be rejected, abandoned and feeling lonely. I can recall a time when I was a babe in Christ actually my first year to where I was in a lonely and alone place and I called on my Heavenly Father for comfort and He came to see about me. He sung a song over me as I felt His tangible touch of comfort upon my heart. As He sung to me I wept and then I brought out with a song myself and it will like this.
I lift my hands to you. Giving you the praise each and every day with you how else can I stay. I lift my hands to you giving you the

Abuse

praise each and every day with you how else can I stay with you.
Lonely moments are struggling times. Its so hard to bare in the season that I try. That I try to stand on your faith with patience in me. But every time I look around there's something differently surround me.
But I lift my hands to you. Giving you the praise each and every day with you how else can I stay. I lift my hands to you giving you the praise each and every day with you how else can I stay with you.
One day I sit thinking to myself. To myself. That I can't believe that I have not yet failed. Because the pressure on my heart. With sorrow daily. Cause every time I take a step up, the enemy makes one with me.
But I lift my hands to you. Giving you the praise each and every day with you how else can I stay. I lift my hands to you giving you the praise each and every day with you how else can I stay with you.

This song brought so much relief and healing to me as I cried and lifted my hands as i sung

Abuse

it. Then when I came around others in this same here in the same I was I encourage them in this song as it lifted them as well. I sung this sung in churches and even sung it at our church talent show at the auditorium to where I won second place and was featured in an article and place on some billboards in Africa.

God has given me many songs as a healing to my soul in my despair times. So many people don't truly understand the severity of emotional abuse and this is why you see alot of kids get affected the most at home by this. Parents its vital to spend time with your kids. Its vital to show them your love, give them identity and be there for them. Parents its vital to show your kids the love you have for one in the house strengthen them as well. Many parents don't understand that separation in the house affect the child and they will evidently react out of that because it will create confusion, divisiveness and the sort. Marriage and local churches especially get attack in this as well but please if you know someone in this state, go to them

Abuse

carry them as if they was your own self and
restore them back until health.

Chapter 24
Characteristics of Love

Love is Patient and Kind

Let's define patient and kind.
-Patient -without complaining, enduring pain, calmly tolerating delay, persevering, diligently submissive, long-suffering.

-kind-gentle, tender, considerate, soft, sympathetic, understanding, delicate and sweet.

Have you ever been in a situation where you had to show love to others even when they wasn't pleasant to you. Well the 1st day of this week of this journey things became drastically terrible. Friendship was disrupted and my friend began to lash out alot about me on the Internet, to others, to my other friends and texted rude messages but I did what the Lord would do show Love inspite of. I was still showing patience and kindness to her without retaliating or gossiping to others about her. I remain focus on the Lord, but it wasn't easy. I had to cast thoughts down and said she knows not what she does. I valued our relationship despite her behaving rudely. After casting thoughts down it just drove me to minister to others through texting encouraging words to others and constantly showing her love by texting her love notes. Then that same week I ran into her at the store to where I spoke to her although she didn't speak to me. I then went to her house because my husband had to minister to her husband. Being there I tried to talked to her but she was nonchalant and became non responsive. Then her kids came in and love on me so much. All the while in my heart I was saying I love you still and I'll wait patiently while you go through this making stage in your life.

Have you truly been patient with one another without complaining or retaliating? If we would truly answer that question it would be probably be, No. I can testify to it. God hates complaining. Lord forgive me for complaining and retaliating. We see this in the book of Exodus where the Israelites exited out of Egypt into the wilderness to the promise land, but they complained which cost that generation not to see the promise land.

Can you truly be kind to others when they are slandering your name and treating you harshly? Yes, flesh may want to rise up with retaliation, but you must discipline your flesh, renew your mind, and give the situation to God. Ask God for wisdom and strength, because you truly will need it. God will reward you for your love and effort. The word of God says to heaps coals over their heads with love and it also says even a fool counted wise when he holds his tongue. After you have done all you can just stand (wait patiently and watch the salvation of the Lord).

Look at the situation of Jesus and Stephen, when they was persecuted they still showed the Love of God. Vengeance is the Lord. Being in a relationship where you value you will be more patient as it develops and mature. Let patience have it perfect works in your relationship.

Love does not envy

Let's define envy.

Envy-discontent and ill over another advantages, possessions, desire for something that another has, an object of such feeling, resentment aroused by jealousy, to regard jealously. ill will, green eye monster, begrudge, covet, lust after, crave, have a grudge against, malice, spite, opposition and backbiting.

This happens alot in churches over position. When one person think they should be in a position and sees another in that position that they felt qualified for and waited for so long over, and then this person that didn't wait as long as they did and don't seem capable of doing a better job than them. So then the set man of the house promotes the other person then you begin to get upset with the set man for looking over you and upset at the person that you felt like took your position. Then you begin to talk about them and bring division and discord in the mist. Being an accuser of the brethren is not of the Lord. This is not the Lord and you must now get delivered from the root of bitterness, rejection, greed, jealousy, abandonment, anger, murder and so on. So let's get rid of envy and embrace what God given you and be faithful over small things and God will make you ruler over much. Please don't envy the wicked one because you see them prospering more than you in materials things, because it will soon come to an end.

Love is not Boastful

Boastful- to talk about oneself too much, with too much pride, bragging, pretentious, bombastic, & swagger.

It's a new trend that's out there now that the young and old alike saying "look at my swagger", but not understanding that this is being boastful and God is not please with it. This is not the characteristics of Love. Bragging about yourself and being someone you're not is not hurting no one, but yourself. This is what hip hop teaches now that to

believe in one own power. This is what Satan deceive Eve with and told her that she will be as like God. Self-Idolizing is an abomination. Put
No other god before him. Let's be careful about every trend that comes out, because it promotes rebellion. This is not Love and we no God is Love.

Love is not Proudful

Proudful- having too much pride in oneself, arrogant, haugthy, great pride.

There's lots of time when flesh wants to rejoice in it own strength instead of giving God the glory. Especially when you have people following you and you prophesy or advise them and they obey it and prosper. Your flesh then would like to take ownership of the person's or situation, but you must remember it's the Lord thy God has giving you power to get wealth and do what you do. This is what happened to Lucifer that's now we no called Satan and our God enemy. God gave him a position over the music department in Heaven as the praise and

Characteristics in Love

worship leader, but he got to proudful in his own ability and gift which the Lord had given him and wanting to be like/as his creator (dummy), he had forgotten it was the Lord that gave him it. He wanted to take the Glory from our Lord, and you know that ain't about to happen. Another story was King Nebuchadnezzar had forgotten it was the Lord that had given him all the fame and fortune he had. So we see that God had to break him down. Then indeed he acknowledge our Lord thy God.

Daniel 4:34-37... After this time had passed, I Nebuchadnezzar, looked up to heaven. My sanity returned, and I praised and worshipped the Most High and honored the own who lives forever. His rule is everlasting, and his kingdom is eternal. All the people of the earth are nothing compared to him. He does as he pleases among the angels of heaven and among the people of the earth. What do you mean by doing these things? When my sanity returned to me, so did my honor and glory and kingdom. My advisers and nobles sought me out, and restored as head of my kingdom, with even greater honor than before. Now I, Nebuchadnezzar, praise and glorify and honor the King of Heaven. All his acts are just and true, and he is able to humble the proud.

Love does not Behave Rudely
Rude- to act crude, rough, too act unkind. Its very easy to retaliate when someone is showing you disrespect, but you must not retaliate by acting rudely.

This is one that's hard to follow, especially when someone is disrespecting you. You can be showing others love, but because of who you represent, who you use to be, gender, or race they still want to disrespect you. You must still show the character of Jesus Christ. There's a time when you to speak and a time when you to speak, but in your timing of speaking you must speak out the spirit of Love. Even in pleading you case or standing up for yourself, you must show Love. The right application for the situation. If you're the one that innocent God will rescue and vindicate, but even if he don't still show the Character of Jesus Christ. If you don't retaliate and ask the Lord for wisdom in the matter he will give unto you, because he is the discerner of the thoughts and intents of man. There are people that is assigned to challenge your character to see if they could throw you off course and to find you guilty by any means necessary. Avoid these types, and choose your words carefully.

John 8:4-10... "Teacher," they said to Jesus, this woman was caught in the act of adultery. The law says to stone her. What do you say? They were trying to trap him into saying something they could use against him, but Jesus stooped down and wrote in the dust with his finger. They kept demanding an answer, so he stood up again and said, "All right, but let the one who has never sinned throw the first stone! Then he stooped down again and wrote in the dust.

Acts 7:59... As they stoned him, Stephen prayed, "Lord Jesus, receive my spirit. He fell to his knees, shouting, Lord, don't charge them with this sin! And with that, he died.

Love does not Demand its Own Way

Demand- to ask for too boldly or urgently without considering the other person, a strong request.

This is the spirit of control in operation. When you not getting things your way. You then begin to operate with the spirit of Jezebel, controlling and manipulation. Stop it I say, and let Love reteach you what he is. Witches does this try to control people will and this is not God. Be confident and secure in who God called you to be. Selfishness only drives people away from you and not to you and you will walk alone not because God got you in the wilderness but because you drove others away. So let Love wash you so you want operate like this no longer. I use to be like this. When I was rejected by my peers, I did began to bully people and make them do I said, but this was Jezebel at her finest and it truly was not the Lord. I wanted to be accepted and love and wanted others to love me, but that was not the way love was suppose be demonstrated. Thank God Deliverance. This happen in marriages so often when the spouse wants his or her way and do whatever it takes to get it. Let's not operate like this anymore. Although Love is a commandment, it still don't forces itself on you to accept it nor show it. It your willingness and obedience to want to humble yourself, obey God commands and instruction.

Love is not Easily Provoked

Easily Provoked- easily annoyed or provoked, excessively sensitive, touchy, easily offended, quick-tempered, resentful.

Proverbs 15:28 NLT... The heart of the Godly thinks carefully before speaking; the mouth of the wicked overflows evil words.

We must be very careful when we hear things. If you have been hurt by someone and you hear certain things, and because the spirit of the root of bitterness is there it because to get stir up. Fear as well began to be in operation and it lead you to get offended by something and it may not concerns you. For instance; when you in a service and your pastor preach a message and you going through a situation in your life you began to get offended. For one, because the pastor knows you, you think the pastor preaching about you, but he's not you just have made a situation bigger than what it is. Jesus said to John the Baptist, blessed to the one that's not easily offended, because offense will come. I use to be this way, getting easily offended by what others say or do to me or what I think they're doing. So let Love teach you how to dust the dust off and move on, and everyone is not against you. Let Love heal you.

Love keeps no Record of Being Wronged

Holding on to the former mistakes and mishaps, harboring passed harsh memories in the heart to bring up for later, storing up old mistakes.

The 1st day of this week in my journey with love does not envy. I went to my friend house and spoke and sat down but the Love was not shown back but it didn't stop me from showing it in return, however, the children came and stole my attention through the whole while we was there and when we was about to leave I said goodbye greetings. My heart was saying I love you still and it wasn't feeling ill toward her. I just wanted to love her more.

The next day I talked to my other friend and she reveal to me what was said about me what my friend that was angry with me had said about me and what she was expecting, and even in that my friend that I was on the phone with me reveal to me what she was expecting from me. This was a hard day with my thought life but I gave it all to God all my heart, strength, soul, &mind how I was feeling misunderstood and the requirements that they was expecting & demanding from me, but I didn't respond bitterly but I apologize and said I was going to try to do my best. If I would have thought about it so hard what was be require on me I would have resented them and retaliated.

Characteristics in Love

I haven't always been like this. The old me would have roused up with retaliation and grudge holding. I would have got mad at both of them.

This week haven't been easy for me, because there were group discussion about me among my other associates, but I remain calm, and gave it to the Lord. It wasn't easy guys, but my love and reconciliation for her still remains. Thank you Lord for Deliverance!

We should never hold on to things of the past. God told us to guard our hearts and renew our minds. You must forgive and let go of that hurt, because it will hinder your future. Forgiveness is a must. Forgiveness releases you to walk in your divine destiny in its full potential, but unforgiveness holds you down. Those experiences is only for you to not return and go through it the same way. Learn from the mistakes and get wisdom out of it, so you can be better next time or forgive them and continue to love them and move on. **To still be a relationship and harbor mistakes of the**

person wrongs in your heart for later is not love, this is nothing but unforgiveness, deep hurt, rejection, resentment, and the root of bitterness and the enemy playground and you are his player. Reject the evil one and truly forgive and move on to destiny. Also if you do this the person that you have supposedly forgiven is unaware of it and they are trying to do better, but because you are harboring grudges in your heart, you want let them move forward and it won't seem like they're doing better because you're blinded by the pass. This put the relationship to a stand still, because u put requirements on them that their not able to do and was not equip to fulfill. Unrealistic Expectation. Deliverance come now in the name of Jesus!!!!

Love Rejoices Not in Iniquity, but Rejoices in the Truth

Rejoice Not-When someone falls short of the glory, you who are spiritual don't laugh or celebrate and say I knew they would. Not to celebrate the mistakes of someone that's weaker than you.

Characteristics in Love

Rejoice in-that our enemy is God enemy and thank God for his vengeance and righteous judgements on our enemies. Rejoices in God's vengeance, because he has vindicated us for obedience towards him when others thought differently and persecuted.

Love Bears all Things
To Never give up no matter what and to carry, to give birth to, to produce or yield, to support or sustain, withstand, to give, to tolerate.

Love Believes All Things
To take as true, real. To trust a statement or promise, To suppose or think, to have trust, faith, and confidence in.

Love Hopes All Things
A feeling that what is wanted will happen, a desire accompanied by an expectation.

Love Endures All Things
To hold up under, to tolerate, to continue, to last, persistent,determines, remains, bears and

Characteristics in Love

stand no matter what the situation or circumstance is.

Chapter 25
Quotes

1. Singles be careful to who you want to marry because if you don't you may spend the rest of your life in regret being miserable.

2. When someone show you that their not interested in you, don't chase them.

3. Being in a neglectful and abandoned relationship is worst than being rejected by others.

4. Ladies never marry a mommas boy because you will always find yourself being left behind and second in his life.

5. Never stay in a relationship where you are in constant begging for attention, appreciation and affection.

Quotes

6. Don't let no man nor woman send you to hell.

7. Some say you will lose your reputation if you get out of that relationship, but I say that you will lose your soul to hell if you stay in that relationship.

8. It takes 2 to build a relationship but 1 to destroy it even with one blow and hit.

9. The thing that you keep running to is really causing you to be enslaved to bondage.

10. Ladies know your worth! Don't settle, because you are feeling lonely. You are far more precious than rubies. Don't let flattery weaken you. Make sure he has substance in him. Make sure he has goals and his plans is to lead you higher in Christ Jesus. Make sure he have goals and plans as a Leader to protect and provide for you.

11. Ladies after you get a prophetic word stating that your husband is coming, don't fall

Quotes

for every man that be presented to you, because counterfeits always comes 1st to throw you off. These counterfeits includes sinner and christian men alike and please by all means don't go chasing after no man.

12. Never settle for left overs.

So remember to Fight as much as you can to keep the God ordained relationship together until there's nothing else left then go a little more further until God says now its time to stop, for you have fought the good fight but it has come to an end.

I pray that you have gain more insight and understanding in reading valuing relationships and hope that this book has impacted your life for the good.. I speak blessing over every relationship that reads this book. May Prosperity and Longevity be the portion of every vessel that reads this book.
God Bless you

www.ingramcontent.com/pod-product-compliance
Lightning Source LLC
LaVergne TN
LVHW051037080426
835508LV00019B/1572